MORE THAN ONE HOMELAND

MORE THAN ONE HOMELAND

A biography of
Commissioner Gladys Calliss

by

FREDERICK COUTTS

Cover design by Jim Moss

Salvationist Publishing and Supplies, Ltd
117-121 Judd Street, London WC1H 9NN

© The Salvation Army
First published 1981
Reprinted 1983
ISBN 0 85412 390 3

GENERAL FREDERICK COUTTS, CBE, Hon DD (Aberdeen), became an officer in The Salvation Army in 1920. He served in corps and divisional work in Great Britain before being appointed to the Literary Department, International Headquarters, where he remained for 18 years and became Literary Secretary. From 1953 to 1957 he was Principal of the International Training College, London, and then became Territorial Commander for Australia Eastern Territory. In 1963 he was elected to be General, in which office he served until his official retirement in 1969. Since then he has continued to serve by the spoken and written word.

Printed in Great Britain by The Campfield Press, St Albans

CONTENTS

ACKNOWLEDGEMENTS

NO biography is one man's work—and this story would never have been written without the indispensable help of Commissioner Gladys Calliss herself. Her own records and memories were freely placed at my disposal, but the responsibility for the final result is mine alone.

I am also indebted to Lieut.-Colonel Melattie Brouwer (R), who is possibly the greatest living authority upon the history of The Salvation Army in Indonesia, and whose detailed story of the *Bala Keselamatan* in *Tanah Toradja* appeared in Australian editions of *The War Cry* in 1973/74. For the service of Enid Lee in Sulawesi I have drawn upon Mrs Commissioner Carr's delightful sketch: *Little Mother Major*.

Thanks are also due to Major Malcolm Bale, our Editor-in-Chief in Melbourne, for his unwearying response to my frequent appeals for photostats of this or that article by, or about, the Commissioner. As they are to my many Salvationist comrades—particularly in Adelaide—who ransacked their memories, delved into corps histories, unearthed ancient photographs, introduced me to 'Little Cornwall', and generally did all in their power to make the past as real as the present. A grateful Pommie warmly acknowledges their help. F. C.

Note. The rank given to officers in this story is the one held by them at the time of reference.

Preface

THE sober hard-backed soldiers' roll of the Colonel Light Gardens Corps of The Salvation Army looked somewhat the worse for wear—but this was only to be expected. The written record of the soldiership of this Adelaide corps had been in continuous use for more than half a century. Nearly as many officers as that number of years had added or deleted names from its pages. In addition, the inside cover bore the signatures of numerous divisional commanders who thus testified that the due procedures for keeping a Salvation Army corps roll had been faithfully followed.

Now and again an Olympian mark can be seen—that of the territorial leader in Melbourne whose eye surveys corps, institutions and divisions alike. But not often does this happen for the Colonel Light Gardens Corps is one of the younger in Adelaide, having been opened on 9 April 1927.

There is one name on that roll, however, which was destined to be known outside the Commonwealth—that of no 35—the teenage Gladys Mary Calliss, who became a soldier on 10 December 1928 during the command of Captain May Millgate. The same name appears a further half-dozen times, carrying the rank of corps cadet, company guard, cradle roll sergeant, primary sergeant, sunbeam leader, guard leader and, in 1933, that of young people's sergeant-major—in more familiar language, the Sunday-school superintendent. Some of these duties were carried out concurrently; others followed in succession; all were undertaken with total dedication. This young woman Salvationist was nothing if not whole-hearted. So none of her comrades in the corps were at all surprised when Candidate Calliss entered the training college for officers in Melbourne early in 1934.

Her name reappeared on the Colonel Light Gardens Corps roll in 1977—this time as Commissioner Gladys Calliss. In one sense in her end was her beginning. But much had happened between those two dates, and it is with these events that this story is concerned.

1

'Little Cornwall'

CLOSE to the western shores of the Upper Yorke Peninsula, with the blue of the Spencer Gulf as a spacious background, lies 'Little Cornwall'—a triangle formed by the one-time busy mining communities of Kadina, Wallaroo and Moonta. Copper had first been discovered in South Australia at Kapunda—45 miles north of Adelaide, and then at Burra Burra—100 miles north-east of the state capital. But the fortunes of 'Little Cornwall' were laid when a shepherd, guarding his flock from the ravages of men and nature, came across a small greenish mound. The following year another shepherd, even less quick on the uptake, stumbled over a pile of copper ore thrown up by a burrowing wombat. He kept his discovery to himself until one day, in his cups, he told a local hotel proprietor who promptly acted upon the information received.

The earlier gold rush to the rich Victorian reefs, and the later settlements on the Western Australian goldfields, undoubtedly made larger headlines, but the copper boom born of the discovery of the Wallaroo and Moonta lodes provided regular employment for more than 60 years for the hundreds of immigrant miners who, with their families, braved the 100 days' sea voyage from Plymouth to Port Adelaide. The grandfather of Gladys Calliss hailed from Lincolnshire but, as a boy of 10, he was brought to Moonta—to be lost among the overwhelming majority whose accents were Cornish, whose social customs were Cornish, and whose religion was one or other of the several brands of Cornish Methodism.

By the end of the century 14 of the 16 churches which could be seen from the engine platform which dominated the centre of Moonta were Methodist in their origin. The practices which prevailed in the old country could be discerned in the new. The bosses worshipped in the Wesleyan chapels; the 'Prims' welcomed the radicals; the Bible Christians were noted for their preachers. The other two places of worship were Anglican and Roman Catholic respectively—but all were shaken when on 12 April 1883, The Salvation Army made its boisterous appearance, led by Staff-Captain and Mrs Thomas Gibbs, assisted by Lieutenant Hayes—an English girl still in her teens, but so attractive that she became known as 'Happy Dinah'. The story is that when she saw Bramwell Booth he asked for her promise that, if he sent her to Australia, she would not marry for at least three years. For how she kept her promise, and whom she eventually married, read on. Meanwhile, the tail-board of a wagon parked on a vacant lot near the Moonta hotel served the three pioneers as platform, and in due course a meeting room was rented in a lane off Ellen Street.

At this time The Salvation Army in Australia was not yet three years old, but the church people of Moonta were generous enough to give the newcomers a welcome—though a leading article in the local paper did make the point that the Army could not expect believers unused to their methods to approve all their peculiar sayings and doings. Nevertheless the Methodist minister did announce that he had read the Army's 'secret book'* and had found that, in the main, the doctrines therein set forth were those of Methodism. The most practical suggestion to be made was that weeknight meetings should close earlier. Young people should not be out and about after eleven o'clock at night.

However, the flame was not to be quenched in Moonta for within three months of the opening of the corps a local lad—the youthful James Bray who had worked as a whim-boy in the mines—left the town to become a Salvation Army officer.

'Whims' were windlasses which were worked by horse power. James and his offsider—for the lads always worked in pairs to make sure that one of them stayed awake—were on the midnight to 6 am shift. Theirs was the task of ensuring that there was a constant flow of water along the half-mile of wooden guttering to the ore crushing machinery. If the whim-boys fell asleep the horse would stop, as would the water supply—until an irascible workman arrived to set boys, horse and water in motion once more.

However, no Salvationist stood upon the order of his going so far as the work of God was concerned. A single question about the need for officers launched this whim-boy on his life's work. His mother sewed a

---

*This was the name given by the critics to the first edition of the *Orders and Regulations for The Salvation Army* which was sold for twopence when published in October 1878. Twenty-five thousand copies were disposed of at this price—so 'secret' was a misnomer.

Lieutenant's yellow braid on his private jacket. The lad armed himself with an outsize, metal Army shield and cheese-cutter cap and left Moonta—though not for any training college. The name of James Bray never appeared on any soldiers' roll, nor did he ever enter any training college. But he remained an officer, revered as one who loved and served his fellow men, until his promotion to Glory in 1951. Perhaps part of the secret was that eventually he married 'Happy Dinah'!

With such a spirit abroad no wonder the Army swept through 'Little Cornwall' as it was elsewhere sweeping through the Australian countryside. The local paper—*The People's Weekly*—was glad to spice its columns with stories of the doings of these newcomers. 'I hear it whispered', wrote one contributor who veiled his identity under the pseudonym of 'Slap Bang', 'that only three barrels of beer have arrived in Moonta this week, and that our police constable's life is one of ease and pleasure now that all the drunks have been reclaimed. It is even rumoured that our hotel keepers are going to commence Saturday night prayer meetings with free beer.'

A fellow contributor, hiding his light under the pen name of 'Tomahawk', declared that everyone in the town was singing the new hit tune: 'So we'll lift up the banner on high'. Store-keepers with nothing to do whistled it. Miners came up the ladder out of the pit singing it. Servants hummed it as they swept the floors. Publicans joined in as well when they thought no one else was listening.

These Yorke Peninsula correspondents had a sharp eye for any peculiar Army practices as well as as a sharp ear for the idiosyncratic Army saying. 'The waving of handkerchiefs', declared one such observer, 'is a novelty. It looks pretty to see a hundred or more waving in the air, though what it means I don't know. The Captain calls it "the week's washing", but to perform this gala act is a test of one's more reverential feelings. But the tambourine knocking is truly beautiful. Only a little more is still wanting—blackened faces, striped trousers and large rolling eyes.' This was undoubtedly 'wrote sarcasticul', as Artemus Ward would have said.

The sayings of some of these converted Cornish expatriates were retailed for public consumption as well. 'Looard', ran one such reputed intercession on behalf of a comrade the results of whose backsliding were plain to see, 'take away our brother's black eye and give 'un a clean 'art.'

A bandsman not wholly satisfied with the sounds which were emerging from his instrument held the bell end to his mouth as he uttered a general commination: 'Looard, if the devil's in me cornet, drive 'un out.'

The corps even rose to the height of an Oswald Pryor cartoon when the example of a well-known local identity, who had been promoted to Glory, was recalled with due benefit of dialect in an open-air meeting. The caption recorded the speaker as saying: 'Listen to our departed brother's dying words: "Bury me in me old red gurensey". At which sentiment a voice from the ringside commented: "Allelooyer! 'E won't want no red gurensey where 'e's gone!"'

But Moonta Salvationists had no objection to their pithier sayings being quoted—or misquoted—when one corps was being opened at the mines and another in the town. A weatherboard structure was built for the first development and a store secured for the second. Even the ranks of Tuscany joined in the celebratory tea meeting which the 'Weekly' reported as having commenced at two o'clock in the afternoon of Monday 29 June, in the presence of 6,000 persons. The figure need not be seriously disputed for detachments from Wallaroo and Kadina travelled in to join the holy feast. A 75-piece band accompanied the singing and, as a crowning attraction, 'Happy Dinah' played the big bass drum. Captain Henry Hancock—by established custom all mine managers and overseers were called 'Cap'n'—was to have presided, but the disappointment felt on account of his unavoidable absence was assuaged by his generous cheque for five guineas. Besides, if one expected guest failed to turn up, were not others being added to both corps weekly in satisfying numbers. And Grandfather Calliss was among them!

He wore a red jacket and, though no Cornishman, was as active as any of the rest in sharing in the open-air meetings which were held wherever two or three humpies had been built together. These were erected on sound do-it-yourself principles. Strips of wattle were nailed to pine uprights and then two of the most able-bodied members of the family, working from opposite sides of the proposed wall, plastered this rough framework with mud and clay which lay in handy heaps upon the ground. Hessian bags were tacked up to serve as ceiling, and then lime and ashes were trampled in to make a floor. Town planning contributed to the lasting dignity of inner Adelaide—but not to Moonta. Fences wound their irregular way among the dumps of slack and the abandoned entrances to disused workings. Apart from the

4

intersecting main streets, a town plan would have resembled nothing more than a jigsaw puzzle.

No matter; the place was prospering. By 1878 at least two government schools, not to mention sundry private establishments, were in operation. In 1885 the foundation stone of a town hall was laid. Before the century was out Moonta could boast the largest population of any centre in South Australia after Adelaide. In 1901 a brick built Salvation Army hall was erected at the corner of Robert and Ellen Streets, and it was here that Arthur Calliss—youngest member of the extensive family of Grandfather Calliss—brought his wife, and here thanks were rendered for their first child, Gladys Mary, born on 23 October 1913. This was the year in which Salvation Army work began in Sulawesi—the island where, as a grown woman, this particular baby would commence her own missionary service.

She can still remember the Sunday evening drive along the flat Kadina road to the hall, as well as the long wooden forms where her parents sat in the third row from the front on the left-hand side. The backrests were covered with white muslin in order to prevent the blouses or shirts of the worshippers sticking to the forms in the fierce summer heat. Sadly the little family was not to be seen there for long. One Sunday the child was thoroughly upset and could not—or would not—be comforted. The exasperated father took her outside and, as can happen, was giving her something to cry for when a tender hearted doorkeeper tried to intervene. 'Don't be too hard on her,' he remonstrated, 'she's only a baby.' Arthur Calliss took this as unwarrantable interference. He thought he knew best how to manage his own child—and never set foot in the hall again, neither did any other member of the family.

Despite more setbacks of this kind which lay in the unknown future, the Calliss family never completely severed their links with the Army. A photograph of Gladys, taken when she had started school at Moonta, shows her wearing a dark jersey and skirt, her shoulder length hair parted on the right side and held in place by a white ribbon. She is gazing intently at the camera. Determination is written in the look in her eyes and the set of her mouth. Resolve might be a better word; certainly not obstinacy. This was a child who was beginning to know her own mind. Well that this was so for she would have to make her own way in years to come.

Happy school days at Moonta were soon to be over, for already there were rumblings that all was not well with the mines. Trade had flourished during the First World War but, with the end of hostilities, the demand for copper plummeted. World markets were glutted with unsaleable ore and the price dropped by half. Three years before the mines went into voluntary liquidation Arthur Calliss moved himself and his family into Adelaide where he found work on the state railways. A timely decision—for on 1 November 1923, at an extraordinary meeting of the mining company in the Victoria Hall, Adelaide, the golden age of Moonta officially ended. All the maintenance services were withdrawn from the mines and any saleable equipment went for scrap.

2

Colonel Light Gardens

BY the end of the First World War the population of Adelaide was approaching 300,000—and was still growing. If ever human judgement was vindicated it was that of Colonel William Light who in 1838 drove the first peg into the ground in order to commence his survey of the open country which stretched out before him as far as Mount Lofty. 'The reasons', he declared, 'that led me to fix Adelaide where it is I do not expect to be generally understood. . . . My enemies, however, by disputing their validity in every particular, have done me the good service of fixing the whole of the responsibility on me. I am perfectly willing to bear it.'

While the First World War was still in progress the South Australian state government commissioned the design of a garden suburb to be built in his honour and to be known by his name. The demands of the war turned the 300 hundred acre site already purchased for this purpose into a giant training camp. This the military authorities did not relinquish until 1920, by which time the increased demand for housing had caused the original scheme greatly to be extended. By the beginning of 1928 over 1,000 new homes had been erected and oc-cupied at an average price of £700 each. As the first large scale suburban development in the state, and with tree lined streets designed to preserve this residential area from through traffic, the name of the 'Colonel Light Gardens' was more than justified. With the help of a low interest housing loan Arthur Calliss secured No 70 Penang Avenue.

He had been living in the Parkside district of Unley, and on Sunday afternoons for months past he and his family had made the 20-minute trudge to see their new home rising from the ground. Gladys would take her brother Alan—two-and-a-half years younger than herself—under her wing, but her eager eye missed no detail of the way in which the family dream was slowly but surely coming true. She saw the one-time farmland marked out in a criss-cross of streets, and watched the workmen grubbing out the deeply set roots of the vines. Then the

7

foundations were laid and the walls began to rise. The shape of things to come became clearer still as she saw how the three bedrooms would be laid out.

Three! Not to mention room for a garden at the front and a vegetable plot at the back, with space for generous flower beds to be planted as soon as the workmen had finished on site, and still boasting sufficient trees to make it appear as if No 70 was deep in the heart of the country. Three cheers for Colonel Light and for the designer, Mr Charles Reade, as well, for his planning of this garden suburb in the colonel's honour.

To add delight to delight, the Calliss family discovered the Army again. The parents had not attended church, nor the children any Sunday-school, since that unhappy day at Moonta, but now they fell in with the Unley Corps whose weeknight open-air meeting was held every Friday evening at the intersection of Unley Road and Frederick Street. Friday night was the late shopping night for Unley, and this progressive corps had changed the venue of its open-air meeting in the interests of a more effective Christian witness—as indeed this proved to be.

In those pre-television, pre-radio days, the Army open-air was an accepted public attraction. Here was light, here was colour, here was music, here was singing—and the Sally Anns never seemed to mind the homely humour enjoyed at their expense. They took it all in good part; in fact, seemed to welcome it—and any heckler who felt he had gone too far could always salve his conscience by throwing a coin into the ring. This was where the sharp-eyed Gladys came into her own. She constituted herself picker-up-in-chief of any coins which rolled off the collection cloth lying in the centre of the ring and so threatening to disappear down an adjacent drain. Half a century ago there might have been grounds for the parody which ended: 'Another elevenpence ha'penny makes the bob.' But every Friday night there was a small girl at Unley who made it her business to see that not even the least of coins was lost.

After Friday evening came Saturday night—which meant another jaunt for the Calliss family, this time by tramcar into the centre of Adelaide where, outside 'The Windsor Castle' and in the shadow of the town hall and the central post office, the Congress Hall Corps held its regular weeknight open-air meeting. As eight o'clock struck Bandmaster Jack Turner would step into the centre of the ring, raise his baton, and the square would be filled with music. The regulars knew that they could set their watches by the Congress Hall Band. In the unlikely event of the town hall clock going crook, there was always the Army open-air meeting which was never late in commencing.

Bliss was it then to be alive—for the next day was Sunday. Gladys and Alan, who by this time was a person in his own right, would listen on a Friday evening to Bandmaster William Baldock reminding the Unley men of the whereabouts of the Sunday morning open-air meeting. Gladys knew the district as well as the next, and Sunday morning would see her and her brother in the appointed street sometimes before the first bandsman had arrived.

Not all had been sweetness and light, however. After the family had settled in their new home, one of the officers at Unley persuaded the Calliss parents to allow their children to attend Sunday-school, promising that they would be called for, taken to the hall, and then brought back again. For this red letter occasion the children had been provided with new clothes—but alas! the promised caller never arrived. Nevertheless Mrs Calliss sent the pair of them off on their own for Gladys knew her way about. The two youngsters waited close to the hall door, growing more and more disconsolate as folk went in and out—but never spoke to them. Finally they dolefully returned home, and that might have been the end of the story.

By this time Gladys had another sister and, one Sunday afternoon, while she was taking care of the new arrival, the family heard the sound of music, music which they recognized. The Salvation Army band from the neighbouring suburb of Goodwood was marching up and down, turning right and then left along the tree-lined streets which intersected Colonel Light Gardens. The Pied Piper of Hamelin was not more persuasive—and the Calliss children could do no other than follow the drum. When the music ceased an announcement was made that Salvation Army meetings would be held in the district as from the following Sunday. There would be meetings for children as well, and a weekly meeting for women. The officer-in-charge would be Captain Hollingsworth, and she would be glad personally to welcome one and all who wished to come to the hall in Kingston Avenue.

Arthur Calliss attended on the first Sunday and the officers visited 70 Penang Avenue during the week. But it was Gladys who attended on the following Sunday, having studied in the meantime a feature entitled 'How to be saved' in a copy of *The Young Soldier* which had been left in her home. Three weeks later, exactly a month after the corps had been opened, the young teenager knelt at the Mercy Seat as a sign of her desire to accept Jesus as Saviour and Lord. Later on Mrs Calliss joined the home league (or weekly women's meeting), and for the first time a Bible was to be seen in the household.

But now even this happy family found their newly-discovered joy clouded by the bitterness of the world depression. Arthur Calliss lost his job and, try as he would, could find no alternative employment— the plight of thousands of other Australians at this time. Gladys had already secured a place at the high school but where was the money for her necessary uniform and equipment to come from? 'Let me go to work', she urged—and she found work in a shirt factory, but before long retrenchment was the order of the day here as well.

In this predicament Gladys made up her mind to accept the first job that came her way and, on the following Saturday, attended a bazaar held in her old school. Up came her former headmaster to ask her how she was faring. 'I finished work yesterday', was her forthright reply. Then the head spoke of one of his friends whose wife had become an invalid and could no longer manage by herself in the home. Would that kind of opening suit Gladys? True to her resolve to take the first situation offered, the girl said, 'Yes'. She began her new work on the following Monday morning and stayed there until March 1934, when she left for the training college, the first candidate from the Colonel Light Gardens Corps.

This was one of the two great blessings of her teenage years. Gladys found herself in a Christian home. The husband was a bank manager and the lady was a child of the manse, a lover of music and, more importantly, a lover of the Lord. Gladys became almost a daughter. Work done, she could roam the library. Almost without being aware of what was happening, her love of reading was deepened. Music was also part of the life of this new home, and so another world of beauty was thrown open to her. She also learned how a house should be run— another lesson which she stored up against those days, as yet unknown, when she would be teaching others.

Yet even in this happy setting inner questionings had begun to arise in her mind concerning officership—a vocation about which she had hitherto felt fully assured. One day she was dusting in the library and the Bible which she was about to return to its place fell open in her hand. One sentence stood out from the printed page. They were words of Jesus, 'Ye have not chosen me, but I have chosen you' (John 15:16). To the young candidate this was a word of the Lord—and she needed no other. So it remained for the rest of her days. When a proposal of marriage would have taken her from the divinely directed path, this word kept her faithful. When on missionary service and an angry crowd harassed her with the cry, *'Pulang orang asing'* ('Go home, foreigner'), the same word kept her steadfast. This was where the Lord would have her be.

The second great blessing along with this development of heart and mind was the opportunity for development in leadership. It is a well-known fact of Salvation Army life that the smaller the corps, the fewer the number of soldiers, the greater are the opportunities for service. It is a blessing in disguise not always to belong to a corps where all is big and bright. So Gladys proved at Colonel Light Gardens. Successive appointments as primary sergeant, sunbeam brigade leader, guard troop leader and finally young people's sergeant-major provided her with abundant scope for youth leadership, handling various age groups in turn.

She learned by doing—the best way of learning. Six successive courses of corps cadet study provided her with a basic foundation of Bible knowledge upon which she built as year succeeded year. No one knew better than she did that these were but the most elementary steps which she was taking to prepare herself for her life's vocation. But at least she was taking them. The same determination with which she had searched for the coins which had rolled into the darkness during the Friday night open-air meetings at Unley was now brought to bear upon her preparatory studies for her life's calling and, in due course, aided by the generous interest of the Christian people whose home life she had shared, she left for the Army's training college at 68 Victoria Parade, East Melbourne.

Interstate travelling in those days was done by train, and the South Australian contingent met their comrades from West Australia on the Adelaide railway station. No-one slept except by snatches on the overnight journey on to Melbourne, and the natural high spirits of the new cadets were further increased as they sighted the slogan painted in large letters on the side of the van which was ready to transport both them and their personal belongings to their new home—'London Baby Carriage'.

The brand new tin trunk belonging to Cadet Calliss was the first to be lifted from the van on reaching the college. To her dismay it was used by the rest of the company as a convenient step to street level. With each pair of feet the dent in the lid was deepened. The owner was too overawed by her new surroundings to protest, but this was not the kind of welcome she either expected or would have chosen.

3

68 Victoria Parade

THE changeable Melbourne climate wore a tolerant face as the members of the Faith Session entered what was called the Federal Training College when erected in 1901 at 68 Victoria Parade. The Commandant, Herbert Booth, third son of the Founder of The Salvation Army, had inspired its construction to make good the loss by fire of the Punt Road training college for men, as well as to provide adequate accommodation for both men and women cadets to be housed in the same building. With its baronial-styled 150-feet frontage and its castellated towers, the building cannot be overlooked even today, and must have looked more imposing still to the cadets who passed through its doors for the first time in March 1934.

The world economic depression was to hang like an unwelcome cloud over the whole of the Australian continent for some time to come, and the Army could not hope to escape what the rest of the country had to endure. Heavy cut-backs were the order of the day. After the Valiant Session had been commissioned at the beginning of 1931, all training was suspended until it was decided that cadets from both territories should be brought together in Melbourne. This arrangement still held good in 1934—which meant that the girl from Moonta met like-minded young people some of whose homes were more than 2,000 miles farther west than her own, or alternatively much the same distance to the north-east.

No matter; this but added to the gaiety of the session. There were 101 of these blithe spirits under the same roof—Bram Lucas, Roy Dawson, Bill Baskin, Florrie Butt, Cyril Whitehouse, Olive Smith, Keith Baker, Enid Lee, Ray Everett—to name only a few, and each was there for the same reason. In charge of them all was Colonel F. H. Saunders, second son of the Edward Saunders who, with John Gore, held the first Salvation Army open-air meeting in the Botanic Park, Adelaide, on Sunday afternoon, 5 September 1880.

All shared the same spartan life so none could complain. Menus

13

were simple—soups and stews were followed by rice or tapioca pudding for afters. Half a pound of broken biscuits was frequent fare for a party in the park on a free afternoon. Amenities were equally limited. A common washroom served all the women cadets. Similar arrangements were all that the men could boast—plus a weekly pilgrimage to the public baths every Friday morning.

But Cadet Calliss had no complaints. She had entered training with but little money in her pocket. Sometimes she was hard pressed for the price of a stamp on a letter home, but this did not prevent her living her days to the full. Never had she known so many public gatherings, nor any so well attended. With many a 'Hallelujah!' her session was publicly welcomed in a crowded Collingwood town hall, and commissioned nine months later in the same building—again packed to the doors. Week after week there were the united holiness meetings in the Melbourne Temple—again occasions of infinite variety. One month the subject was 'Browsing in the Psalms', another 'Spiritual Arithmetic'—both handled by the training principal, and always an expectant crowd. Nor was Calliss herself above carrying a billboard bearing some directly worded Bible text, though she was inwardly embarrassed at times when, thus burdened, she tried to sit down in a Melbourne tram.

There was much to do within the college walls as well—in the matter of Bible study, for example. Cadets were required to follow the time-honoured method of beginning at the beginning of the appointed textbook and continuing steadfastly without a break to the end. This meant that the ground between Genesis and Revelation was covered in upwards of 100 seven-leagued lessons—with another equally substantial series on Christian doctrine to follow. Almost without time to draw breath came those multifarious regulations which covered the corporate activities, as well as the individual lives, of Salvationists themselves, officers and soldiers alike. Nor was there any perceptible slackening when, in open class as well as in private study, cadets travailed in heart and mind to construct a Bible address upon a chosen scriptural incident or theme. Such material as had been thoroughly prepared had then to be adequately delivered—hence the agonizing hour known as 'field drill' when, in a pre-microphone age, cadets were taught how to speak—both out of doors as well as indoors—relying solely upon the unaided human voice though, as a concession to human frailty, a megaphone could be used if and when available. Nothing was deemed to be impossible in training. If required, an attempt would have been made to teach crows to sing.

14

Though at this date The Salvation Army in Australia was only 54 years old its history was not to be overlooked, for in certain ventures it had outpaced the work in the land of the Army's birth. Among these were the establishment of a counselling service for prison inmates; the opening of reception centres for discharged men prisoners and a similar institution for women; the provision of statutory care for young people in moral danger; the establishment of reformatories for boys; the acceptance of responsibility for neglected children and the provision of low cost accommodation for the travelling public. The success of these various initiatives persuaded William Booth to send Major T. Henry Howard to Australia to make a first-hand report upon all this specialized work. 'The child (Australia)', said he, 'has outgrown the parent (England)'.

Facts of this order were meat and drink to every Australian cadet—and certainly to Cadet Calliss. Her final report described her as having 'done good work in first and second classes. . . . Satisfactory advance has been made'. More significantly, there was 'further capacity for development'. Equally noteworthy was the fact that her fellow cadets rated her as highly as did her leaders. 'She has a mania for work', was one of their comments in the sessional magazine, and she was photographed for 'her cheerful smile'.

Before the session ended one of the training college staff suggested that her sense of dedication might be strengthened by a text from the promise box. She agreed, and the text which she took read: 'Seekest thou great things for thyself? Seek them not'. This but confirmed her own bent of mind, for when she was required to give the main Bible address in the afternoon meeting of Commissioning Sunday on 6 January 1935 she chose the declaration: 'O Lord, truly I am thy servant' (Psalm 116:16). The cadet who sat next to her in class was to remember that address more than 40 years later.

The War Cry of that date referred to her 'clear exposition of the obligations of a servant of Christ', though at the time no one saw any significance in the fact that the opposite page of that same issue carried an account of the return of another single woman officer from a second term of service in the Netherlands Indies. Probationary Lieutenant Calliss was to be a servant but, at the start, in a very different role from the one usually prophesied for her. At her commissioning she was appointed to the training college house staff. Her mother was not altogether pleased about this. She thought that her girl should have been given a 'better' posting. But the new

15

Lieutenant's reaction on returning to 68 Victoria Parade was to hurry into the kitchen and to cry joyfully: 'I'm the first of the Faith Session to arrive at my new appointment'.

For the next two years this large room with its flagged floor, bounded on the one side by the men's quadrangle and, on the other, by the women's, was to be her world. Across one end lay the two dining halls, to which separate hatches gave separate access. Alternate fortnights on kitchen and laundry were to be her lot for the first 12 months. When in the second year she was placed in charge of the kitchen there was some opportunity to share in the actual training of the cadets, but the wonder was that anyone would have had any energy to spare for such additional duties.

The day began at six o'clock with a call on the cornet. At times some bright lad thought he would improve the early morning hour by playing 'Home, sweet home', but the kitchen officer had no time for such sweet thoughts for she had to see that the cadets on duty cleaned out and kindled the 'bobby' so that hot water would be available for domestic purposes. The principal item of kitchen equipment was a large flat-topped stove with fireplace in the middle, a series of ovens of varying sizes on either side, and a complement of pots and pans on top. Heating and cooking was by solid fuel—mostly briquettes.

Outside the kitchen door lay the grease trap into which flowed the waste water from sinks and gutters. The iron lid had to be lifted each day save Sunday, the trap scoured out, the lid black-leaded and replaced. With wry humour this primitive sanitary device was known as Jacob's well. Laundry duty was no sinecure either, for this embraced all the personal effects of both men and women cadets, together with the pillow slips, sheets, blankets, towels, curtains, tea-cloths and every other washable item in the college inventory.

When her probationary term was over the second year's service was no lighter, for upon the Lieutenant—now confirmed in that rank, fell the task of preparing the college meals according to the prescribed menu—and this at a time when ready cash was in short supply and the price of groceries and greens was rocketing. Calliss did her best to brighten the dinner diet of 'depression stew', as well as to cheer the tea table with some welcome dainty. In her spare time she would haunt the local cake shops in search of any new confection she could economically copy, and studied the menus in the city cafeterias to discover how simple meals could be presented more invitingly.

Ultimately the hard-working kitchen officer had to be replaced and, on medical advice, was appointed to the drier and warmer climate of Western Australia. First came two short appointments as second officer to Bunbury and Kalgoorlie respectively, then promotion to Captain with responsibility in succession for Buckland Hill (later known as Mosman Park but now closed), Wiluna (now closed), South Perth (now known as Bentley) and Highgate (now known as Balga).

The second of these was a test of any officer's mettle—particularly that of a single girl with but three years' experience. Wiluna was a mining town which had known better days, situated in an arid area nearly 800 miles inland from Perth. The ground was barren for miles around. Stunted bamboo shrubs were the only vegetation that would grow in the savage heat. The Army girls were two of the very few women who remained in the place the whole year round. Of fridges and freezers there were none—and the tin hut which served as hall, with a couple of rooms at the back for quarters, did nothing to make life more bearable. There was but one adult male soldier at Wiluna, and most of the time he was absent rather than present. Yet that year the corps won the territorial efficiency shield for all round progress in youth activities. The young people's legion which the Captain personally supervised provided the lads and girls of the district with their sole form of organized recreation—and she was to reap her reward many years later.

In 1972 one of the heads of the Australian Embassy staff in Jakarta was checking a list of his compatriots living in Indonesia when he halted at the name of Calliss. A faint bell rang in his mind. As a lad at Wiluna he had known an Army officer of that name. His father had been on the mines management, and he himself had found a cultural and spiritual haven in what had been styled the young people's legion, nothing ultra highbrow, but certainly a boon and a blessing in that isolated township. Could there be any link? The next embassy reception set his mind at rest. 'My old Sunday-school teacher' was how he presented the Chief Secretary for The Salvation Army in Indonesia to the other guests.

The education of the children of officers serving overseas is frequently a cause for concern, and that year there was a family of three young Australians in the Indonesian capital in search of such provision. To see that this need was met rested upon the shoulders of the one-time lassie Captain at Wiluna. The need was to be met by the former youthful legion member at Wiluna—in that year chairman of the board of governors controlling the joint embassy school in Jakarta. Not for the first time, nor the last, was Calliss to find her bread, cast upon the waters, returning after many days.

With this flair for work among young people, Captain Calliss was later appointed as youth leader for the Western Australia Division, and then served for three years in the same capacity in Northern Victoria with Bendigo as her divisional headquarters. This country area brought her the widest opportunities she had yet known. At a time when car travel was limited, she did most of her frequent journeys by train, rising early and returning late, but rejoicing in the youth camps and weekend house parties and refresher courses where faith was confirmed by facing each problem as it arose. Promotion to the rank of Adjutant was followed by a transfer to similar work in Western Victoria, with headquarters at Ballarat.

By this time the Second World War was over and the tightly woven web of Salvation Army communications, torn to shreds in a hundred places, was being laboriously pieced together. Officers who had been interned were making their way home. These two circumstances were to change completely the course of the life of the 33-year-old youth officer. She was unexpectedly to see a current copy of the international *War Cry*. She was to meet Major Melattie Brouwer, on homeland furlough from the Netherlands Indies.

4

Pacific pilgrimage

AT this time of day it would be hard to say which of these two facts influenced Adjutant Calliss the more. In mid-1946, when the lifting smoke was revealing the gaps left in the Army's ranks by the war, the international *War Cry*—still cut to four pages weekly because of continued paper rationing—was running an inch and a half square panel headed: 'The General asks—who answers?' Then followed an enquiry of not more than 20 words from various overseas leaders in areas where the work had suffered most severely. At the foot of page one of the issue for 25 May 1946, the question read: 'Who is there to help? Must I write again about the need for more officers?' This Macedonian cry was signed by Gerrit Lebbink, Chief Secretary for the Netherlands Indies. 'But when I read it', wrote Calliss afterwards, 'I felt an almost physical pain in my heart.'

On the way from Ballarat to Geelong where the following day's youth councils were to be held, she tried to banish all thought of the Netherlands Indies from her mind. But among the guests for the weekend was the newly-returned Major Melattie Brouwer, daughter of a Dutch father who had been one of the two principal pioneers of the Army's work in Java in 1894 and an Australian mother who was appointed to the same Dutch colony five years later. Melattie herself was born in Semarang and, thanks to the various appointments held by her parents while she was still in her teens, was fluent in English, Dutch, Malay and Chinese. A deep sense of vocation possessed this gifted officer who, though trained in Holland, was appointed to Java in 1928, and continued to serve in Indonesia until her retirement in 1964. Like the rest of her expatriate comrades she suffered the hazards of invasion and was interned from December 1942 until October 1945—only to find that the campaign for Indonesian independence which ensued held as many perils for them as occupation by the Japanese. No one could speak more eloquently about the needs of the country than Melattie Brouwer because no one was better informed. Over the weekend Gladys Calliss heard the story often.

There were further youth councils on the following Sunday at Ballarat, and in the meantime the troubled youth officer tried to list the reasons why she should forget all about overseas service. Up to this particular moment she had never wanted to become a missionary. Nor to exchange life in her beloved Australia for life in any other land, however alluring. And at the moment the troubled Indonesian archipelago was not exactly alluring. In any case, she was already deep in studies which would make her still more qualified to serve where she was. Was there any sense in robbing Peter to pay Paul?

Some additional delegates arrived unexpectedly for this particular weekend, and Calliss had to take two of them into her own quarters. This meant that she had to sleep on the floor of her living room—a fact mentioned only because it was that floor which became her altar. As the final meeting of the day was drawing to a close a young woman stepped forward in an act of dedication. She was known to Calliss— and known as one who was burdened with a sense of vocation which she was unwilling to accept. So the unwilling candidate was counselled by an unwilling missionary. When we cannot see our way—was the advice given—we should trust and still obey. What the younger woman agreed to do set a pattern for the older, whose own act of dedication was made by her makeshift bed on the living room floor. Next morning the youth officer told the divisional commander of her resolve and, having set down her intention in writing, left for her annual furlough with a quiet heart.

The Adjutant returned from furlough possessed by the strongest possible assurance that her offer of overseas service would be accepted. Eager to make certain that the thinking of her immediate leaders agreed with what she felt sure was the Lord's will for her, she asked for an interview with the Chief Secretary, Colonel Wilfred Kitching— subsequently the Army's international leader from 1954 to 1963.

'I am going to Indonesia. I am learning the language. Nothing will stop me', she announced. Such determination could not be gainsaid, and when the seventh General with Mrs Kitching visited the newly-independent country in 1961, it was the one-time youth officer who shared in the meetings and helped in the task of translation into Bahasa Indonesia.

Of all this she then knew nothing. Meantime comrade officers pointed out that no one had been sent from Australia to Java for a number of years. No matter; she was going! Others emphasized the unwisdom of committing oneself to a country where conditions were far from settled. All too true: the red and white flag of Indonesia was hoisted on 17 August 1945, but not until 29 December 1949 did the Netherlands government agree to a complete transfer of power. Even then dissident groups continued their own private struggle against the newly-recognized national government. But the hazards of an unknown future were not to turn her back. Her life was committed to Indonesia but, above all, it was committed to God. Her faith would not fail!

But what about essential equipment, was another enquiry. Not so serious a problem as some anticipated for this missionary candidate believed in travelling light. Two small trunks would carry such worldly possessions as she wished to take with her. Simplicity and utility governed her choice of linen and clothing. Purely ornamental items were deemed superfluous though, as a concession, she included part of a dinner set. A few treasured books were included, as well as sundry pots and pans—but there was no point in being buried beneath a mountain of luggage. Far more important was what could be carried in her head, not to mention her heart, and that was why she had started on a course in Dutch.

Soon the days began to fly past with increasing rapidity. Her passport was called in for the necessary visa, and returned stamped 'Celebes'. Then came word of her appointment—divisional secretary in the Central Celebes Division to assist Lieut.-Colonel and Mrs Leonard Woodward. Gladys took a deep breath. This was better than ever she had expected. Better than she deserved, she felt. The Woodwards were missionaries cast in the Livingstonian mould. He was an English country lad who first met the Army in the Shropshire town of Ironbridge, and entered training at Clapton in 1903. He married Margaret Low, a girl from Perth, in May 1915 and within less than 15 months had arrived in Java. By April 1917, they were in Sulawesi (as the Celebes became known) where in the central area there were already three centres of Salvationist activity. West of the Palu river were the Danish Captain and Mrs Jensen; the Dutch Ensign and Mrs Veerenhuis were in charge of the farm colony at Kalawara; a day's journey on horseback further up country were the Dutch Captain and Mrs Loois at Kulawi. Kantewu, which the Woodwards were to pioneer, was a further three days' journey—one on horseback and two on foot. This, so he had been told by his territorial commander, would be the centre of his work in an area of roughly 150 miles by 80 miles which was without a single Christian missionary.

This called for faith, mighty faith, for Woodward did not even know the local language—Oema, though some of the Kantewu men understood Moma, the language spoken in Kulawi where Mrs Woodward remained while her husband explored their far-flung parish. For some time he lived in the *lobo* or village temple at Kantewu, which also served as a primitive hostel for visitors. The principal 'religious' practice of the people themselves was head-hunting—a custom born of the superstition that a man's soul was in his head. The only way in which the evil spirits who inhabited the soil could be persuaded not to hinder the growth of the crops was by burying as many human heads as possible in the ground. In this macabre setting the Woodwards laboured for four years before rejoicing over their first two converts. This was the area to which Calliss herself was to be appointed.

For the moment her concern was how to reach her destination. Normal commercial shipping was in disarray. In sympathy with the Indonesian claim for national independence the Australian waterside workers were refusing to service Dutch vessels. But there were irregular sailings to Singapore—at least a move in the right geographical direction—and Calliss found an experienced travelling companion in the Australian Major Rose Flood who had escaped across the Chindwin River when Burma was overrun in 1942 and who was now returning to Rangoon. The fellowship of that voyage helped to prepare the apprentice missionary physically, mentally and spiritually. Calliss used her skills as a youth officer to provide material which Major Flood could use among the young folk in Burma as the work opened up again, at the same time profiting from all that the more experienced woman could communicate from her own overseas service.

They had to part company on reaching Singapore, and for Calliss there were further delays waiting for a Dutch ship bound for Java. But waiting time was not wasted time, for she found herself in the company of the heroic Bertha Grey and Elsie Willis who had continued to operate their girls' home for seven and a half months after the city had surrendered to the Japanese. There was always work in which Calliss could share—in the girls' sewing room, for example, which helped to keep the home solvent; at the Army meetings in Clemenceau Avenue; in selling Army literature in the hotels and restaurants; in sharing the low key street patrols when girls in need of food and protection could be discreetly advised where these could be found.

After several weeks a passage was secured, and one torrid summer day the long-suffering traveller disembarked at Jakarta. Scanty as was her personal luggage, it was too much for the still scantier dockside transport. One of her precious trunks had to be left on the quayside for later attention. Meanwhile she was to report to the territorial headquarters at Bandung, but as the road via Bogor was cut by sporadic fighting, the journey would have to be made by plane—in this instance that war-time packhorse of the allied air forces, the DC3. Comforts there were none in that multi-purpose utility craft. And few friends either—for the newcomer could not understand a word of what the other passengers, inelegantly strapped around the sides of the plane, were saying. Then the pilot and co-pilot clambered aboard, exchanging witticisms in the broadest 'strine'. Their anxious countrywoman relaxed. This she did understand—and her fears fell away.

Major Brouwer was waiting for her at the other end, for she had not remained at home for a moment longer than was necessary. Java was written more deeply on her heart than Calais on that of Mary Tudor. Her one consuming aim was to gather together the flock that had lacked a shepherd's care during the disorder and destruction of the war, and her sister officer sought to be possessed by the same desire. No more than any other Army property was the territorial centre exempt from the horrid marks of war. The cadets' lecture room had been used as a detention centre for suspects and the walls, bespattered by bloodstains, bore grisly witness to the nature of such interrogations.

Back in Jakarta there was more cleaning for Calliss to share. The building now known as Jalan Kramat Raya 55 had just been placed at the Army's disposal in lieu of another which had been taken over by the police, but as this exchanged property had been occupied by the allied forces it was like any other where troops had been quartered—in need of a thorough cleansing from roof to floor. Calliss continued to display her expertise with bucket and scrubbing brush. Walls had to be washed down; windows to be cleaned; floors to be scrubbed several times over before they were rid of ingrained filth. Little did she dream that this particular building would become the territorial training college where she herself would serve for 11 years—three in charge of the women cadets and a further eight as principal.

But apron, bucket and scrubbing brush had to be returned to store at the news that there was a sailing due to leave for Sulawesi. This was only to Makassar on the south-western tip of the island—where there was yet more delay which once again Calliss tried to put to good use. She found food and friends at the Army's maternity home—in effect a solitary overcrowded house which had survived the calamities of war, mainly because the Swedish Brigadier Esther Petterson was the matron. As a neutral she had been allowed to continue to serve in her professional capacity. Her own story was something of an epic in itself. Years previously she had lost an arm in an accident, but with her own left hand and an artificial right one had pursued her calling with undiminished competence. To meet yet another dedicated spirit was a further inspiration to the visitor who was soon to embark on the last and briefest of her several voyages. For two days the *Bontekoe* nosed her way northward and then hove to about half-a-mile to sea off Donggala—the somewhat drab mid-Celebes seaport lying just south of the equator. But as the local shipping agent's motor boat drew near, Calliss picked out two smiling faces—that of the Finnish Major Juutilainen and that of the Indonesian Adjutant Sahetappy. Luggage was no problem now—reduced as it was to one trunk and a suitcase. Once on shore, there was a woman officer to greet her as well—the German Adjutant Esther Karcher whom she was to replace.

These various officers who had greeted the newcomer on her chequered way across the Pacific were themselves a witness to the indestructible unity of the Army in the service of human need. During the Second World War they had been tested as severely as any of their other comrades in the Far East. By reason of their nationality some had been free throughout the entire period of the Second World War and, in spite of ever-dwindling resources, had continued to act as servants of all. Others had been interned but later, with the Japanese advances, had been freed. A large number, free to begin with, were later interned. But no change of circumstance gave rise to any personal bitterness. Those who were free did what they could to help those denied their freedom. Men and women of half-a-dozen European nationalities maintained a Christian spirit towards one another as well as to those who were not of their race or their faith. It seemed to Calliss that these were of the company of the Lord's anointed and that this, at long last, was her promised land.

The coast road which she took around the bay to Palu was certainly full of beauty. Part of a mountain range towered steeply above the head of the gulf. Richly feathered birds flew in and out of the bright green foliage. Clusters of palm trees lifted their pencil straight trunks into the clear blue sky, while more immediately overhead multitudes of butterflies of every hue gyrated in a pattern too complicated for the eye to follow. Yet the roadside altars with their gifts of fruit for the spirits, and the bits of rag fluttering on the end of a bamboo cane to draw attention to these offerings, spoke of a darkness which was as opaque as the daylight was bright.

Palu was a centre of local government and a trading town. The simple Salvation Army property in the place had been put to uses sacred and profane. At one time it had housed a clinic which carried out a merciful work in an area where disease was rife and genuine remedies rare. During the occupation the place had been turned into a brothel, but once again it was a house of Christian worship and service.

Through the open door Calliss could see a table laid for a meal and, as she sat down with her new comrades, staring eyes peered through the windows and inquisitive faces filled the doorway. A white woman was a rare curiosity, but if the uninvited spectators wished to see a white woman eat, Calliss had no objection. It might help them to realize that she was just as human as they were. In any case, she had already made up her mind to accept whatever was placed before her, whether she liked it or not. Rice seemed safe enough. Tomatoes with onion—in moderation—might not be too much of a risk. But she had not been warned that the dishes had been liberally flavoured with red-hot chillies. Her first mouthful brought an anticipatory gasp from the onlookers and, as her own eyes and nose began to water, Calliss felt as if burning pokers had been laid across her tongue and were forcing their way down her throat.

'She will soon speak our language', observed some of the company sagely. 'See, she can eat our chillies.' The new divisional secretary was not sure on either point. In the event she was to shed more tears over language than the chillies.

Fortunately the remaining 20 miles to the divisional centre did not take long, and the new arrival was not sorry when she heard the driver say: 'This is Kalawara'. It took her less time still to encompass the facilities provided by her new headquarters—a solitary dwelling house raised on tree stumps. On the left of the front verandah, reached by a short flight of steps, stood the divisional office lit by a single kerosene lamp. Level with this low verandah but to the right were the sitting room and bedroom which the Woodwards made their home. Behind the divisional office was the room which had been occupied by Adjutant Karcher where Calliss herself would now live. Behind that again was a communal dining area, marked off by a waist-high fence but innocent of mats on the floor or decorations on the walls. Further steps

25

led to a covered gangway and the kitchen, washroom and storeroom, together with the simplest of accommodation for any visitors. From there another path led across a stream to a rudimentary toilet.

This was life stripped to its barest essentials. To have come thus far was a test of determination. Sterner tests lay ahead.

5

Kalawara

LIEUT.-COLONEL WOODWARD was away on one of his divisional rounds when his Australian reinforcement reached Kalawara. He had waited for her until he could wait no longer, so delayed had she been by time and tide. A six weeks' tour of one of the remoter parts of Central Sulawesi could not be further postponed. But Mrs Woodward was at home to welcome the newcomer in her own warm-hearted fashion. She had not forgotten how she herself felt when first she arrived in Sulawesi 30 years previously. Even with her long experience behind her she was still not entirely at home on the narrow bridle paths which clung to the precipitous mountain sides, nor did she care to peer down into the ravines whose depths were hidden in perpetual shadow. She had no desire to greet at any time any of the numerous members of the snake family, nor was she ever wholly reconciled to the presence of the lesser creepy-crawlies. She did not relish the days, still less the nights, when her husband was away from home, but none of this could be inferred from the affectionate smile with which Gladys Calliss was greeted. Remembering how difficult she had found it to hold the simplest conversation with the women closest to her, she had made up her mind to help this new single woman missionary to avoid some of her own early embarrassments.

First of all, the language. Five new words each day would be the minimum target. For example: plate, knife, fork, cup, spoon. Nose, eyes, mouth, teeth, ears. Sun, moon, dawn, sunset, stars. Pray, kneel, sing, stand, read. Arms, legs, hands, fingers, feet. Eat, drink, wash, sleep, wake. Each morning would see a list begun and, by God's help, each evening its close. The first five words were not hard to remember, but the first 25 could leave the learner confused.

But there were other aids than learning by rote. Family prayers were held each morning in this home-cum-headquarters. From the start Calliss had to take her turn in reading the Bible portion, though for a time she was allowed to pray in English. As there were usually two or three trainee candidates working on and around the divisional property there was always a ground-swell of conversation which enabled Calliss to become familiar with the everyday sounds and phrases of the new language.

This still left her to grapple with the work of the divisional secretary—the prosaic task which she had been given. To begin with, there was the cash book, and a basic Salvation Army rule the world over is that every penny received has to be accounted for. Had they been pennies the new divisional secretary would have found her work easy. But they were not; they were rupiahs and cents—a currency with which she was not familiar, and both bills and receipts were in a language which she was still trying to learn. The same difficulty applied to the correspondence. How file letters which could be in Indonesian, Dutch or English? And how does one understand letters in one or other of these languages which are already filed away?

The change of climate and food added to the sternness of this discipline. Calliss herself had never been anything of a weakling. Her strong physique and ready will had enabled her to go through a full day's work—and then be ready for the next. But no expatriate could escape the effects of the heat and humidity of an equatorial climate, not to mention the recurring bouts of dysentery and fever. Calliss was near to tears as she read again the line in her song book: 'And what if strength should fail?'.

The regular meetings would have been more of a help had she been able to enter into them more fully. Even the singing was not the inspiration which it had been to her at home. The harmonies were not discordant. Pacific melodies had a haunting beauty of their own. It was just that they were different from those which she had known from girlhood and from which she could still draw refreshment when she sang them to herself. Even the prayers did not always speak to her condition. They were earnest enough. That she realized from the tones in which they were uttered. But that was not the same as fully understanding them—and not fully understanding she could not fully respond. She longed for a fellowship into which she could freely enter instead of struggling to share.

Of course the Woodwards themselves were a present help in any time of need. The Colonel returned from his divisional journeyings about three weeks after Calliss had arrived. Just as she had felt at home with Mrs Woodward from the moment they had met, so she quickly fell under the spell of *Tua Janggu* or 'the bearded one'. In Sulawesi

28

beards were accepted as a sign of wisdom, and Woodward was genuinely blessed with the inner discernment to which a beard was believed to testify. Mrs Woodward had already made the new arrival feel that she was wanted, and had gone out of her way to pass on to her such domestic knowledge as she herself had gained the hard way. Cookery was an altogether different art when baking was done in a kerosene or biscuit tin laid across a couple of bars underneath which was kindled a fire of scrub wood topped off by pieces of coconut husk. Beancake was a welcome change from rice, but the soya beans had to be soaked for days—usually in a basket lowered into the river—and then the womenfolk would tread them out with their bare feet. Both meat and potatoes were treats. One had to learn that while some leaves were poisonous there was a bracken fern—a kind of vegetable—which could be cooked and eaten. Sweet corn and cassava (tapioca root) often appeared on the menu, though the Indonesian people much preferred rice. There were always bananas and paw-paw—not forgetting durian, a fruit which conceals a pulp tasting (it is said) like a rich vanilla ice cream within a hard prickly skin. Against indulging in durian was its pungent smell. Mrs Woodward would not have the fruit in the house, but her husband was so fond of it that he would hide it in an office cupboard, to which he would resort at convenient intervals.

Calliss shared his fondness for durian. Perhaps that was an element in her appreciation of him as 'the most wonderful missionary I have ever met'. The truth was that his bronzed and bearded figure, of above average height, his lively eyes often gleaming with the joy of living, and the unforced laughter which often possessed him, endeared him to all who met him. He was a prince among men when it came to Christian encounter. He could talk to the people of Sulawesi as one of their number—as indeed he had been since the days of the First World War. He could be a Toraja to the Torajas with the same divine ease that a Paul of Tarsus was a Jew to the Jews and a Greek to the Greeks. True he was not enamoured of the paper work which can clutter up a divisional office in the east as in the west. But he saw to it that Calliss was shown her way around even though a typewriter was a rare luxury and lighting was by oil lamp. More importantly, he made sure that she was introduced as speedily as possible to the task of strengthening the Toraja Salvationists in their most holy faith and, under God, of adding to their number such as should be saved.

Once a month the divisional bullock cart made the journey down to Palu to collect the teachers' salaries and rations from the government authorities. (At this time there was no state education as now understood so a primary school was attached to each corps. How could children learn of Jesus unless they could read about Him? Schools were an integral part of the work of God.) As there were no shops in the mountain areas the villagers would also rely upon whoever was going into town to bring back any essential commodity which they needed. This could be sometimes sugar, or salt, or soap, or a length of calico. The cargo was always a mixed one. Now and again a man teacher would want a pair of new sandshoes—whereupon a broad foot would be placed firmly on the cover of an exercise book and the outline roughed out in pencil. Feet were broad because the men had never worn shoes until they had come of age.

Calliss had done this trip before—but always with another officer. Now it was thought that she was experienced enough to go on her own, helped by a couple of lad trainee candidates—one of whom was Celsius Merpati, currently the divisional commander for Java, with headquarters at Semarang. The lads made ready the bullock cart—a de luxe model with rubber tyred wheels taken from a discarded motor car, a canvas top and a slatted bamboo floor. The oxen were yoked while Calliss wrote out what she would have to say: 'May I have the rations for the teachers.'

The outward journey was uneventful but when 'Miss Australia'—as Calliss had become known—made her first call in Palu, a small crowd gathered. By the time she was making her last, the few had become many. A young white woman in Palu was a rare sight; no one of that colour could go unnoticed. But Calliss put on a brave face as if this was all in a day's work and, gripping her slip of paper tightly, said to the attendant: 'May I have the rations for the teachers, please?'.

The attendant, whose name was Jonathan, looked blankly at her, as if he had not a clue as to what the strange visitor was saying. Calliss repeated her request but, with an indifferent air, Jonathan answered: 'I do not understand English.'

The impasse meant only one of two things. Either he was being deliberately obstructive or else Calliss could not make even the simplest request in his own tongue. The onlookers began to stir and edged more closely about the two principals involved. Then a man's voice called out: 'She is speaking Indonesian, Jonathan. Listen to her.' Once again Calliss asked for the rations and this time the attendant, the blank look on his face unchanged, pushed across the table the items required. The tension relaxed. The crowd fell back. The boys from Kalawara silently loaded the goods on to the cart and, hot and humiliated, Calliss walked along the road by their side. How often was she to be mortified in this way?

Never when she was going by bullock cart with the Colonel to some Salvation Army mountain centre, nor when on a more extended tour with Mrs Woodward and himself. This was the kind of travel where the immaculate navy blue uniform with its crimson trimmings, so familiar in the western world, was discarded as unsuitable because unserviceable. Photographs from this period show that Woodward wore a khaki shirt and trousers and a bush hat. Calliss wore a short sleeved, open neck khaki shirt with skirt to match. Orthodox readers will be reassured to learn that washable 'S's' were also worn. But much can be allowed to a divisional commander who could enjoy a night's sleep on the unyielding floor of a bullock cart while his assistant officer unrolled a mattress, pillow, sheet, blanket and mosquito net and made up her bed in a corner of the hall behind a makeshift screen of palm branches. In the morning there was always the swift flowing mountain stream where each could wash in turn.

Calliss described one such visit in an article which later appeared in the Australian Salvation Army youth paper *Victory*.

At present I am on tour with Lieut.-Colonel Woodward and have arrived at a village called Bomba . . . There were 117 people on the floor of the front verandah for a meeting in the afternoon. Near the garden gate, about 20 feet away, is a small river in which we have to wash. We stand on stones at the edge of the water and do our best.

We travelled 22 miles yesterday by bullock cart, at a pace of three or four miles an hour. Two boys travel with us and look after the bullocks. It is a thrill for these young people to go on tour with the Colonel. They take part in the meetings and act as translators when necessary. There are seven languages and several dialects in this division, but I have to learn Malay for the people and Dutch for the business contacts and records.

At the end of the meeting there were 12 seekers. I was particularly interested in an intelligent looking girl who appeared to be very concerned. . . . I learned afterwards that her father was a Moslem and her mother a spirit worshipper. This acceptance of the Christian faith in front of all these people would be a great test for her. She had told the Captain's wife some time previously that she wanted to accept Christianity. She needs our prayers.

We left at seven o'clock the following morning for another village about 10 miles away, but as the road was so rough and we had to cross about six creeks it was 11 o'clock before we arrived there. . . . For a meal we were given cassava. Someone brought a coconut and others brought eggs and vegetables. The Colonel had a tin of real Australian camp pie with him. This we shared, and it tasted just as good as roast turkey.

When a more prolonged tour was planned, preparations were more detailed. Mrs Woodward had a baking session and then made rusks from some of the loaves. Bedding was aired and the three piece mattresses wrapped in a khaki sheet and grey blanket.

The Colonel would inspect his simple medicine chest and replenish his stocks of iodine, aspirin and ointments. He did not pretend to be a male nurse, still less a doctor, but clinics were few and far between in these remote parts, and his seasoned eye was worth more than all the local spells put together. To his simple remedies he would add toys for the officers' children, pictures and sweets for the boys and girls who came to the meetings, needles for mothers and grandmothers, pieces of soap for the menfolk and reading material for himself. On this point Woodward must have felt himself akin to Wesley who used to declare that no horse ever stumbled while he was riding and reading.

As for Calliss, she would make ready the inspection reports and have on hand any correspondence which could be better dealt with by an on the spot conversation than by further letter writing.

The programme varied but little from village to village. There were always goitres to be painted with iodine and aches to be rubbed with ointment. No one who was sick went away without some comforting word. Children were taught an Army chorus and told a New Testament story. Converts were encouraged in their new-found faith. Officers and local officers were instructed how better to feed the flock of God. Few in the village but benefited from the visit of *Tua Janggu*. As one old warrior said to Woodward: 'If your Jesus is anything like you, I could love Him.'

One other major advance in which Calliss shared before the departure of the Woodwards for retirement in England was the recommencement of training work at Kalawara. For this purpose Major Melattie Brouwer came over on a short visit from Java so that the venture might profit from her experience. As all the cadets except one were from the three Sulawesi divisions and as there was no college in operation in Java at this time, it was natural that the cadets should be trained on their home island. The widowed Major Mrs Elna Poutiainen, who was already responsible for the farm colony, was entrusted with this additional responsibility as this was where the

32

cadets were to be housed. As has so often happened, this enterprise was restarted on a shoestring. Part of the existing property at Kalawara was used for the cadets' dormitories, dining room and assembly hall. The divisional trio were added *en bloc* to the teaching staff—though not, of course, to the neglect of their existing duties. *Tua Janggu* helped with the principal's lectures and Bible classes. Mrs Woodward dealt with the home league and other women's interests. Calliss taught subject notes and drew on her experience of youth work in Australia. She was now on her way to a mastery of the language which eventually would cause not a few Indonesians to suppose that she had spoken it from childhood. Her breakthrough occurred when, at a youth council, she had dealt with a young girl who had come to the Mercy Seat. To her unbounded joy she discovered that what she was saying was understood by the seeker and was used by God to her acceptance of Jesus as Saviour and Lord.

Because of the shortage of finance the cadets themselves had to work beyond the normal call of duty. Classes were limited to mornings; afternoons were reserved for work on the land colony. The men cadets gathered coconuts as the kernel, when dried out, becomes copra which can be used as a base for coconut oil. The leaves of the palm, woven in simple mat fashion, can serve as thatch for roofing and fencing, while the dried leaves and stalks are useful as firewood. Softened in water and then beaten, the thick husk provides a fibre which is employed in floor covering or rope making. The women cadets gathered coffee berries and ground maize. Some of this was work to which the cadets were not normally accustomed, but it is noteworthy that, with one exception, all the members of this session who were commissioned gave at least 25 years' unbroken service as Salvation Army officers.

These additional duties may have been a blessing in disguise so far as Calliss was concerned for they took her mind away from the fact that the day of the Woodwards' farewell was steadily drawing nearer. Officers and friends came from far and near to honour them. Government representatives sang their praises as loudly and long as the soldiers and converts who had been their spiritual children. The Colonel's response was characteristic. He chose as his farewell text Luke 6:26: 'Woe unto you, when all men shall speak well of you!' He also asked that a substantial portion of his final allowance should be paid in newly-minted one cent coins. Calliss accompanied the two of them to Donggala—as did five of the hillmen who had served them in various personal ways. As the truck carrying the Woodwards passed through the villages down to the coast the local folk gathered for a last tearful glimpse of their Army leaders. The tension was broken when the Colonel showered them with his newly-minted cents, and more often than not tears were forgotten in the scramble that ensued.

At the port the ship was standing out to sea but Calliss and the five men were rowed across in a canoe. They sat silent and still for this was a new experience for them. The sea itself was new and the mechanism of the ship itself was new. But when the siren sounded and they realized that this meant a final parting they broke out in loud lamentation. In vain did Woodward try to quiet them, so he came to the head of the gangway and, with Calliss at his side, said: 'Your mother and father have to go home to England, but we leave with you a big sister who will love and help you in our place'.

6

Land of the mountain and the flood

THE retirement of *Tua Janggu* left a large empty space which no one but another *Tua Janggu* could fill, but as his work—or rather God's work through him—had to be continued, the Finnish Major Mrs Poutiainen from the nearby farm colony was appointed as his successor.

The new divisional commander had much going for her—total dedication for one thing, for earlier she had buried her officer-husband in Java and then her only child in Sulawesi. Nor did the language present her with any difficulty but, though her spirit was willing, at the end of nine months she was given other responsibilities in Java. The division was then divided into three districts, each in the care of an Indonesian officer, with Calliss remaining at Kalawara to oversight the general administration.

Something of what this entailed will be told in what follows, but any signs of immediate help were not discernible. One of her fellow cadets from the Faith Session—Enid Lee— was appointed to Kulawi towards the end of 1951 and, after 14 months there, took over the medical centre at Kantewu. Half-way through 1952 another Australian girl, Captain Melva Trembath, was appointed to the divisional headquarters at Kalawara where she served for a year. In the interests of easier transport Salvationists in Australia were to send across a landrover, but by the time this arrived Calliss herself was in Bandung prior to leaving for her own hard-earned homeland furlough. Meanwhile she soldiered on by herself.

Early and welcome visitors before Mrs Poutiainen farewelled were the Chief Secretary of the Indonesian Territory, Lieut.-Colonel Derk Ramaker, and his wife. As the only officer in the area whose first language was English, Calliss felt an increasing longing to hear more of her mother tongue. Overseas posts arrived but once every three weeks. Radio was not commercially available. Such papers in English as reached Kalawara were usually three months later than their date of publication. But Mrs Ramaker was an Australian officer and her husband, though Dutch by birth, was also at home in English, so Calliss looked forward to a free flow of uninhibited conversation.

Councils had been planned for the officers at the mountain corps of Kulawi, but the day previously the all-purpose truck which was to convey the divisional party broke down. Hastily a man was dispatched to Palu for aid, but the necessary spares were not in stock nor could an alternative vehicle be hired. As most of the officers would already have left their village corps for Kulawi the meetings could not be cancelled. In this emergency oxen were borrowed from friendly sources in Kalawara and the divisional bullock cart was made ready for the first 15 miles of the uphill journey. No distance at all in western eyes—but four to five hours at least at bullock pace. One of the lads who served on the divisional headquarters was sent off in advance on the horse which Calliss often rode in order to make ready a fire and prepare a hot drink at Talakona, the first halt. About two o'clock in the morning the chief secretary, the divisional secretary, the divisional commander— Major Mrs Poutiainen—and Calliss, with a young man Lieutenant to drive, set off in the darkness. Conversation flowed freely in Indonesian, Dutch and English until, around seven o'clock, a cheerful fire was sighted on the edge of the road. A tin of water was soon boiling merrily, and the bread and margarine, hard boiled eggs and hot black coffee never tasted so good.

For the remaining 10 miles the divisional commander took the horse while the chief secretary and Calliss stepped it out on foot, talking of many things, and Kulawi was reached about noon. Half an hour later there was a sound which could only be that of an ancient car in travail. Sound was confirmed by sight as a vehicle of venerable age rounded a bend in the road. The doors were tied with rope and, in the front seat, looking anything but comfortable, sat Mrs Ramaker. Some Indonesian well-wishers in the valley below were anxious that she should not be deprived of the fellowship of the meetings and so, almost against her will, they had coaxed this ancient of days into newness of life. With equal faith in the Providence who neither slumbers nor sleeps, the entire visiting party returned to Kalawara by the same vehicle. That the number of involuntary stops on the homeward journey did not exceed a total of eight was gratefully accepted as a crowning mercy.

The closing months of 1949 was a time of increasing tension for the Indonesian people. For them the war did not end with the cessation of hostilities in the Pacific in August 1945. The Japanese hold upon their islands, reaching for more than 3,000 miles across the Pacific, might

36

have been broken but there was scant desire to accept the Dutch back again, even if the country had benefited in some ways from their rule in the past. None were more exercised in heart and mind on this point than the expatriate Salvation Army officers who were there simply because of their desire to further the highest interests of the people of Indonesia.

At such times rumours sprang up in a night and perished in a night. Various dates were announced in turn for Independence Day—and then cancelled, but on the evening of 16 December came word that an Indonesian President had been duly elected and the national flag of red and white would be raised the following day. Officials in jeeps, messengers on bicycles, runners on foot, carried the good news from village to village, and at Kalawara the finishing touches were given to the flag that would be unfurled at six o'clock in the morning.

By common consent the European divisional leader had usually been the leader in any community celebrations in the village, but this time Mrs Poutiainen felt that she should give place to the local headman. However, the flag-raising ceremony was held in the grounds of the Army school. All Salvationists were happy to echo the call for national unity and, as might be expected in a land where God is worshipped, shared in the desire that His blessing might rest upon the new state. The people were about to leave for their homes when a voice called out: 'Are we not going to pray?' 'Yes', came back the answer from someone else in the crowd, 'let the Major pray'—and with that silence fell upon the gathering as the divisional commander besought the God and Father of all men to bless and guide the new nation.

Ten days later an Army contingent from Kalawara was present for the flag raising at Biromaru—the centre of one of the several 'kingdoms' into which that part of Sulawesi was divided. Though this was a predominantly Moslem area, so that the service was led by Moslem clergy, the Army flag, Army uniforms, Army sounds and, most importantly of all, the Army spirit was manifest. Among the 1,000 school children present were four flute bands from nearby mountain corps and, as the divisional youth secretary, Calliss rejoiced when amid the medley of sound she could pick out 'her' flute bands by the music they were playing. One of their favourite tunes was the newly-acquired 'Stepping on together in the ranks of truth'.

As the melody was coming over the air one of the Moslem community leaders remarked to Calliss that the village from which the youthful players came had been one of the worst in the 'kingdom' in times past. The inhabitants feared neither God nor man. With their blow pipes and poisoned darts they could defend themselves against all comers—even troops of the Dutch forces. His own grandfather had been killed in this way. 'But then', continued the speaker, 'two of your own men managed to get into the village, chatting with the people from house to house, telling them of your religion until they believed—and were changed.'

It was with renewed faith that Calliss went home that night. Those who sowed in tears would reap in joy. She had need of that faith now that she was to be on her own, for one of the heaviest demands upon her physical and nervous strength arose from the hazards of constant travel. Not only did she carry the care of all the churches but the additional burden of getting from church to church. In the first century the Apostle Paul enjoyed the blessing of Roman roads. There was no equivalent to the Appian Way in Sulawesi. The choice for Calliss in the 20th century lay between the springless bullock cart, or riding her horse, or walking—and walking through the night was less exhausting than in the fierce heat of the day. Even a lift in a jeep could prove a mixed blessing.

At one time when Calliss was on her own at Kalawara the authorities advised her that it might be wiser to go to and from Palu by jeep when collecting the salaries and rations for the teachers. The approved technique was to hail any vehicle coming up from the coast and arrange for a lift down to Palu on the return journey at night. On this occasion it was near to midnight when the jeep—already carrying 16 men—pulled up outside the divisional headquarters. There were loud protests from the existing passengers at the thought of increasing their number. But salaries and rations would wait for no man. What was more, the driver had given his word and, though he could not take the girl who usually accompanied Calliss on such errands, room would have to be made for her. Eventually she sat with her legs dangling over the back of the vehicle.

The road cut through some dense jungle country and a cry arose for the driver to halt. Some of the men felt sure they could replenish their domestic larder by catching possibly a wild pig. Some argument ensued but the motion was carried. The jeep halted, decanting the 16 Indonesians and the one white woman into the pitch darkness of the forest road. The hunting party disappeared; the less adventurous—including Calliss—waited with such resignation as they could muster. Mercifully it was not long before the prey, securely trussed, was flung into the trailer and the passengers remounted. In due course the dawn broke and Calliss could see more clearly the kind of company she had been keeping. At the officers' quarters at Palu she drank more hot black coffee, persuaded that with the Lord the darkness shineth as the day.

Other journeys could be more exhausting because of treacherous ground conditions. Tropical rains, landslides, flooded rivers, fallen trees left no alternative to foot-slogging. Of course, in reasonable weather a day's march could cover anything from 15 to 20 miles. From Kulawi to Kalawara, or vice versa, was an overnight walk—which meant a start at nine o'clock in the evening and a dawn arrival at the other end, allowing for a couple of breaks for hot black coffee made at the side of the road by the young trainee candidates who were never happier than when accompanying their divisional officer and attending to her needs.

On longer journeys the little party would sleep overnight on the way. At intervals along the roadside was to be found a primitive kind of travellers' rest—a roof of palm leaves supported by young saplings—which provided simple shelter for food and sleep. Long practice perfected a regular drill. One of the boys would kindle a fire and, having drawn water from a nearby stream, would bring it to the boil for the inevitable black coffee. One of the girls would cook the ration of rice which the travellers carried with them, adding certain wild leaves known to be edible and nourishing. A simple yet satisfying meal could be made in this way of rice and what might be described as a variety of wild cabbage cooked in coconut milk, with the half shell serving as a plate. For the epicure there could be added a savouring of chilli with a slice of onion and wild tomato. Then with a mat beneath and the protection of a mosquito net overhead, an uneasy doze might follow.

So simple a life-style had its irritations—the segmented worm commonly known as the leech was one example. Any leech could be guaranteed to find its way through a lace hole in one's shoe or a button hole in one's shirt, and any human wading through shallow water was an easy target. If necessary a leech could judge its fall from an overhanging branch on to one's cheek to a nicety, and the success of one such effort was of the greatest encouragement to the rest of the tribe. The victim could be attacked simultaneously or seriatim, and unless preventive action was taken without delay the initial wound would become an ulcer, and the ulcer result in a permanent scar.

Various counter offensives could be tried. A sprinkling of salt was deemed to be efficacious, as was a lighted match. Calliss herself carried a short length of bamboo filled with soapy water, and a quick anointing could prove an effective deterrent. At the same time she declares that to this day she bears on her body the marks of past conflicts.

Bridges—high and lifted up—were another hazard for the traveller. Some would rise and fall as the wayfarer progressed from the nearer to the farther bank. Others would sway from side to side. The more ill tempered accomplished both feats at once. Facing one such river crossing Calliss waited until one of her sure-footed boys took the horse over and then, with the rest of the party, crossed the 20-yard contraption of loose planks and straggling wire on hope and a continuous prayer.

On another occasion she halted at what passed for a bridge but which looked so flimsy that her own weight would be enough to submerge the middle section under the swiftly flowing stream. Yet it was the only means of crossing the river for miles on either side. Her dilemma was solved when two men, each carrying a stout stump apiece, waded into the water. They breasted the current until they stood in midstream and, propping up the drooping structure on either side, waited for Calliss to pick her careful way across as if on dry land.

Hazards such as these could tax the traveller to the point of exhaustion. One particularly inaccessible appointment entailed a two-day journey on foot for incessant rain had made it impossible to use either beast or vehicle. The rough ground played havoc with the shoes which Calliss was wearing. Emergency repairs with wooden insoles enabled her to reach the final descent to her destination where one of the officers, armed with a spear to ensure a foothold on the muddy slopes, preceded her while another, similarly equipped, followed behind. Between them they brought their visitor to the comparative safety of the floor of the valley.

As might be expected conditions in so isolated an area were straitened. Even rice was a luxury. The main item of diet resembled a large white potato. Any kind of animal life was so highly prized that it was not uncommon for worshippers to bring a piglet or two to the meeting, wrapped in the thin blanket which was all the owner possessed to keep himself warm. But the fellowship of the weekend's gatherings more than made up for the peril, toil and pain of the journey. The corps officers asked that their infant son should be dedicated—and to this Calliss gladly agreed. The substance of this simple service is the same wherever the Army flag flies. No elaborate ceremonial. No expensive robes. No sprinkling. The parents simply give God thanks for entrusting them with a new life and ask His help in bringing up the child in the fear and admonition of the Lord. The congregation signifies its assent to the prayer offered, and it is noteworthy that this particular prayer has been abundantly answered. The baby boy is now a Salvation Army officer, married to a capable officer-nurse. They are primarily evangelists but, in addition, their school work has had such an influence on the children in their care that parents have benefited from what has been taught in class, and the basic teaching in elementary hygiene given in the clinic has made a perceptible improvement in public health.

There was still more for Calliss to do on this trip. The next port of call was a new opening at which a recently-commissioned officer was stationed. This meant another overnight stop at a roadside shelter, then a dawn start which brought the visiting party to its destination by noon. Despite the fact that most of the people in this valley knew but little about the Christian gospel—a form of spirit worship had long been the traditional cult—the new arrivals were made welcome. A sleeping place with a measure of seclusion had been prepared for Calliss and an equally 'private' bathroom had been ingeniously constructed out of palm branches embedded in a shallower section of the river.

As darkness fell the congregation gathered under a roof of palm leaves. Night among the mountains could be chilly even in the tropics, so a fire was kindled for light and warmth. But those present seemed apathetic. When they sang it was without enthusiasm. In any case, they did not know many Salvation Army melodies. And when an appeal was made for those who would accept Jesus as Saviour and Lord, there was no response whatever.

The young officers in charge of the infant corps were greatly disappointed. But the meeting was hardly over when the local chief and some of his henchmen asked whether another meeting could not be held before the visitors took their departure. He and his people would remain where they were. Calliss could rest as long as she wished. Some of his men would keep guard so that she would not be disturbed. When she was ready to commence a further gathering they would be waiting.

Dawn was breaking as the second meeting began. It was destined to make good the disappointments of the first. The son of the village chief was brought for Christian dedication. The word of life was read. A gospel appeal was made. Before the meeting ended all who were present had signified their desire to accept Jesus as Saviour and Lord. With gladness in her heart and yet aware that these people were but babes in Christ, Calliss commended them to the God of all grace and to the loving instruction of their own officers.

Thus began one of the longest—and possibly one of the most taxing—days in her life. As no one could remember a white woman ever having visited this village before, the two men officers—with spears—resumed their dual role as guide and guard for the first few miles. The boys who were with her strapped the party's personal luggage on their backs, and another young couple who were candidates for officership joined them for the journey home. Some short way along the road there was a break for the customary coffee. A fervent prayer was offered by the wayside. The men officers turned back. Calliss and her party pressed on.

All the while heavy tropical rain was steadily falling. As mile succeeded mile Calliss grew even more wet—if that were possible, and more weary—which she certainly was. The sharp ferns which grew on either side the narrow track were cutting her face and arms. The leeches were particularly venomous. The long day wore on and then, as darkness fell with its usual suddenness, she felt she could go no farther. The events of the previous days and nights had drained her of strength. On previous tours she had always been able to put one foot before the other, but now she begged the young couple to go on without her.

For answer the young wife, who had been carrying her baby, took the pole to which their clothing, their food supplies and their cooking pot had been fastened. With his free arm the young husband supported his leader while with the other he carried the lamp. On they trudged until they came to one of the roadside rest houses. There, wet and chilled, they waited until a clearing sky enabled them to continue their journey and to find, on arriving at the next corps, a refreshing meal of fried rice and the essential hot black coffee.

There was food for brother soul as well as brother body for, during the family prayers which followed, some favourite Indonesian verses which spoke of giving thanks to God for everything were sung. At the line which can be paraphrased: 'And thank You for the thorns as well as the flowers', Calliss could not restrain her tears.

A few of the more experienced officers in the division commended her because it had been known for one or two of the white men officers to need carrying down that stretch of mountain track. 'You are', they said, 'just like a man!' Calliss was not so sure. The implication—unintended no doubt—was that in some way a woman was not equal to a man. Without entering into the pros and cons of so futile a debate, Calliss had no wish to be a man. She was more than content with the state to which God had called her. But she knew what they meant, and in her heart of hearts was not displeased.

Happily not all journeys were so taxing. A number of the corps were much more accessible and others were better organized so that it was not unusual, on approaching a village, to be greeted by a flute band made up of Army day school pupils. In such circumstances Calliss was not infrequently saluted with the British national anthem. After all, was she not English speaking? And a woman? What was amiss then with 'God save the Queen'? The distinction between royalty and commoner and the even deeper difference between Australian and Pommie is not fully comprehended in all parts of the world. But Calliss was always ready to take the will for the deed, especially when the next tune to fall on her ears was 'Joy in The Salvation Army'. No doubt about that!

7

'And can I be dismayed?'

THE declaration of Indonesian independence, proclaimed on the morning of 17 August 1945, was signed by Sukarno (first President) and Mohammed Hatta (first Prime Minister) in a matter of moments, but the new republic was assailed by fightings within and fears without for many months to come. More than four years were to elapse before sovereignty was formally transferred by the Dutch government in The Hague to the new government in Jakarta. Meanwhile, and even thereafter, there were those who, having done battle against their colonial masters, were loath to forego the power that lies in the barrel of a gun. There were island groups strung across the Pacific from Kotaraja in north-west Sumatra to the border with Papua New Guinea in the east who saw no reason why their own communities should not enjoy an independence similar to that claimed by the central government. There were other factions whose aims were based more on an economic ideology than a national ideal. And, as often is the case, there were also the freebooters who hoisted the skull and crossbones by declaring that everything—literally everything—was now up for grabs.

Sulawesi had its share of this turbulence. Nor was it to be expected that The Salvation Army, little more than 30 years old in this part of the world, should have the measure of these conflicting groups, each with their separate declaration that their way—and theirs alone—was the way of salvation for their country. But at least Calliss and her comrades knew where their duty lay. Their constant aim—in fair weather as in foul—was to preach Christ to the people, to live like Christ among the people and, in the name of Christ, to serve the people. Hence though often perplexed, they were never in despair; though persecuted, they did not feel themselves forsaken. Happily for their lone leader, she had already found a retreat in the very mountain village (mentioned earlier) where the people, at one time so ungovernable, had been transformed by the witness of a couple of

44

visiting Salvationists. Once again the Christian leaven had done its own blessed work.

At some bygone date this particular height had been an active volcano but now was shaped like some giant hollow tooth, with the village homes dotted around the edge of the crater. At one vantage point the local comrades had built a simple shelter with a roof of palm leaves supported by four saplings and furnished it with a seat. Here the eye could find ample delight for the look-out commanded a view of the valley below through which the river wound circuitously like some giant snake uncoiling itself. Here nothing but the cry of birds and the buzz of insects broke the silence—a welcome change from Kalawara where every sound penetrated the thin walls of the divisional headquarters from dawn till dusk. To complete these natural delights there was a 'private bathroom' whose main amenity was a hollow bamboo fitted into the course of a mountain stream so that ice-cold water cascaded over a platform where the occupant was hidden from view by a shoulder high screen of—you've guessed it—palm leaves. In this fastness the visitor could read, and rest, and return to duty restored in body, mind and soul.

Well that this was so, for guerillas from the south of the island crossed the mountain passes and invaded the central belt where the Toraja people lived and Calliss worked. Livestock was killed and eaten. Stores of rice and coffee, made ready for the market, were plundered. Salvation Army halls and school buildings were ransacked and burnt. The villagers went in fear of their lives for the marauders, meeting little opposition, swept on as far as Palu. At one point an officer, two teachers and two corps cadets were kidnapped—though for what reason Calliss was not to know for several years.

Standing one afternoon on the front verandah of the training college in Jakarta, waiting for a brigade of cadets to return from duty, she saw a man hesitate at the entrance and then come up to speak to her. He explained that he had just been released from prison and had been given a boat ticket back to Makasar. He confessed that he had once been involved in the kidnapping of some Salvationists in Sulawesi. No harm had come to them, for all their captors wanted was the help of some translators who knew the local dialect which they themselves could not understand. But what had impressed them was that their prisoners had prayed not only for their own families and friends but for those who had abducted them as well. To round off the story, the one-time guerilla had attended a meeting in the prison where he had been confined which was addressed by a young man officer from the training college. With a plate for his meals, a sleeping mat for his bed at night, and a prayer that his future might be happier than his past had been, the unexpected visitor was sent on his way.

Long before this, however, Calliss had been compelled to face up to the events to which this story was but part sequel.

One Sunday, after the holiness meeting had been concluded, there was the unusual sound of a horse being ridden at a gallop into the village. The messenger carried a warning that Dutch officials in the neighbourhood had been taken captive by the rebels who were now on their way to seize Calliss and her European comrade officers.

Emergency arrangements were hastily improvised. The senior Indonesian officer was placed in charge of the divisional headquarters and given the keys of the safe. The lads who were working on the headquarters were told to take the two girls serving there back to their home village along with Lemuel—the horse that Calliss rode. Unaware of what might await her, she filled a case and a kit bag each with a Bible, a sheet, a mosquito net, malarial tablets and a change of clothing. By this time the girls who were to return to their village were sitting on the floor, sobbing, and holding tightly to one of her uniforms. It seemed as if panic was at hand. Then Calliss remembered that the unwelcome news had so caught them off guard that they had forgotten to pray. She turned into her own room and closed the door but, before she could even commence to frame a prayer, the word came to her: 'Do not be afraid. Nothing will harm you'—and with that the peace of God possessed her heart.

As Calliss opened her door to speak this word of reassurance to the woman officer who was with her at the time, she herself was waiting outside to say that this was the message which had just come to her. And when the two of them went together to the nearby farm colony, the manager met them along the road with the news that this was the comfortable word which had been received by him as well. Then Calliss remembered that this was the opening day of the congress in Melbourne—in the territory which she had left to come to Indonesia. Without doubt some of her own comrades were remembering them before the throne of grace in prayer. Later a jeep was heard coming up the road but, as they waited for its arrival, the sound died away. Then word came that the village chief and some of his headmen had been parleying with the rebel envoys. The Salvation Army people were good people was what they said. Far from doing harm to the neighbourhood they were among their best friends. They cared for the needy and

46

taught the children in the day school. They should not be molested. The village needed them and would stand surety for them. A car engine started up again—but the vehicle was being driven off in the opposite direction.

But Calliss had not finished with these well-intentioned if troublesome irregulars. General and Mrs Orsborn were to reach Indonesia in June 1950—a very important occasion indeed for no international leader had visited the country since General Evangeline Booth in 1937. A delegation of 50, made up of officers, school children and a flute band, were to cross from central Sulawesi to Java to greet them. But how to get off the island when opponents of the central government in Jakarta were in power in Sulawesi? In addition, there was to be the first international Salvation Army youth congress to be held in London, and a young Toraja delegate, Jusuf Rungka, was waiting for his travel documents to be approved.

Fortunately Calliss discovered that she knew the insurgent leader in Palu, and the good offices of an Indonesian woman doctor in the district secured her an appointment with him. Even the journey to Palu had its hazards, but Calliss covered her head like a Moslem woman and finally was led through the tight cordon of his guards armed with their sharpened bamboo spears. In the event the situation proved to be of the hard shell, soft centre, variety. By now Calliss was conversationally fluent and could discuss business with facility with any official, so that it was easier than she had thought possible to gain the needful permission for the Army party to leave for Java.

Two hired trucks conveyed the mixed company of adults and children, together with three overseas officers who had been serving in the interior, to the point of embarkation. Thanks to a flotilla of canoes all were able to board the Dutch vessel anchored off-shore—only to be halted next day at Makasar. The word was now all change. There was a war on in south Sulawesi as well. All through the night intermittent firing had been heard off-shore. In vain did Calliss and Major Sahetappy, who was accompanying the party, plead their cause with the ship's captain and show once more the travel documents blessed by Palu. The right hand did not want to know what the left hand had done. He himself could take them no further, but he could say that he had heard that there was a possibility of a cattle ship sailing from Makasar to Java, via Bali. But, even if they secured a passage, they themselves would have to arrange for the trans-shipment of their party and their luggage though, as a sign of his goodwill, he would allow the

Salvation Army company to remain on board until the two of them returned.

The white Australian woman and the dark-skinned Indonesian made an unusual pair as, during a lull in the firing, they hurried along the sandbagged road lined with armed men. It needed only one apprehensive soldier to let off a single wild shot for the general firing to recommence. Resisting the temptation to run, the two Salvationists kept up a smart pace to the local shipping office where they made their wants known without delay.

Fifty people, adults and children, were seeking a passage to Java.
'How many?'
'Fifty'.
'When?'
'Now! the sooner the better.'
'With the present troubles, impossible!'
'But is there not a cattle boat sailing for Java?'
There was—carrying pigs.
'But if pigs, why not passengers?'
'You don't mind the company you keep, then?'
'Not so long as we get to Java.'
'Very well. It leaves in an hour or so. You'll have to see to your own luggage.'

The two of them hardly stayed to express their thanks. But on the way back they remembered that those whom they had left on the boat from Palu had not eaten for many hours, so they paused long enough at a street food stall to buy up the entire stock of fried bananas. As for the luggage, they happened to meet a local Salvationist who willingly offered to help with its conveyance—with the happy result that in due course the entire party was sailing with the pigs to Java. To crown all, sailing via Bali, a pleasure for which the pampered western tourist is willing to pay heavily. This particular Sunday was Whit-Sunday, and it is not hard to believe that He who is known as the Comforter or Helper was befriending His otherwise friendless flock.

A few days later the Salvationists from Sulawesi were overjoyed to be listening to their General and he was more than happy to see them. Of this meeting he wrote in his autobiography, *The House of My Pilgrimage*: 'At Surabaya, as our plane alighted, we were greeted by a large and excited crowd of our dear people. A boys' band from a former head-hunting district in the Celebes rendered musical honours on home-made instruments.' There was every reason for the excitement. The Javanese comrades knew of the unrest in Sulawesi and had almost given up hope of seeing the visitors. To see the General was more like a dream than a reality to the folk who had crossed the water. The whole occasion was an immense encouragement to the national officers and soldiers who had endured the Army being proscribed, and then their country riven by rival factions so that their last state was almost worse than their first. But to feel that they belonged to an indivisible Army, and to hear their international leader say, 'Our flag can fly anywhere. It unites all nations and changes enemies into friends', was a powerful spiritual tonic.

The group from Sulawesi had need of all the encouragement they could be given, for the voyage home was another nightmare. Once again the entire party had to trans-ship at Makasar—only this time the delay lasted 14 days. The Army's maternity hospital was giving way at the seams, and Calliss thought herself fortunate that a Norwegian officer-nurse shared her own improvised accommodation with her. Most of the other members of the party slept in a disused fort near the seashore, and a meal of rice and vegetables was provided twice a day from a local restaurant. At long last a ship ominously named *The Black Dog* was ready for sailing. In addition to the civilian passengers there were several hundred soldiers on board on their way to put down the rebellion in Sulawesi. A few expatriates were offered third-class accommodation which was neither desired nor desirable. Others slept in the ship's lifeboats. Most remained on deck where, despite the frequent showers, life was preferable to down below. Eventually they all came safely to land.

There were economic storms to be faced as well—the devaluation of the currency by 50 per cent being the most serious of these. The unorthodox—but entirely effective—method of accomplishing this was by cutting a note in half. The portion which carried the figure of the Dutch Queen was not negotiable. The other section was worth half its printed value.

Towards the end of the month Calliss had to make the customary trip by bullock cart to Palu to collect the teachers' salaries and to undertake the neighbourhood shopping. But she reached the government offices to be told that there was no money. The new currency had not yet arrived. The inevitable chaffering ensued. If the schools were to be kept open the teachers must have their money. To refuse to pay them would only harm the children. Could she not be given some of the old half-size notes? They would do for the time being. To which the answer was that if she insisted on this she would have to cut them herself. With that a clerk emptied a pail of five-gulden notes on to the table. And when Calliss protested that she had no scissors with her, she was given a pair of nail scissors—small, blunt and rusty.

Hours of weary work lay before her. Palu is almost on the equator. The heat and humidity can break the spirit as well as exhaust the body. Calliss cut—and cut—and cut until her forefinger was blistered and the perspiration running down her face made it hard for her to see what she was doing. But she could not leave the dusty office until the last of those notes had been divided. As her weariness increased so did the rebellion in her heart. Was work such as this an integral part of her vocation? Could she not be as fruitfully—indeed, more fruitfully—employed in Australia, where at least she could enjoy those normal creature comforts to which any human being is entitled?

The task completed, she left the office and began to walk along the road to the Palu bridge. This was another part of the district which she did not like. In keeping with ancient custom human heads had been buried in its foundations. But as she crossed the river a fresh breeze stirred the leaves on the banana trees. It was a wind from the sea. It was also a wind of the Spirit for it brought back to the discouraged officer the promise of her candidate days: 'Ye have not chosen me, but I have chosen you.' It was enough! That was the spirit of willing acceptance in which Calliss knew she would serve. 'Just where He needs me there would I be.' So be it!

The wind of the Spirit brought other encouragements—even through an ancient hand-operated gramophone playing the old 78s.

In one remote quarters a Toraja officer asked her what she had missed most while serving as a missionary officer in Sulawesi.

'Salvation Army band music', she replied.

At this the officer left the room—to return with an instrument which, said he, had been given him some years previously by Lieut.-Colonel Woodward. It could still be wound by hand, he explained, and he himself had made the existing needle out of bamboo. He had only two records, he added—showing Calliss one of them.

'March—"Flowing River",' she read aloud 'and one of my favourites for as long as I can remember. There are words to this march

50

as well, and the songster brigade at my last corps in Australia used to sing them. I know every bar of this piece', she added excitedly.

Opinions may vary as to whether whistling is, or is not, a desirable feminine accomplishment—but Calliss used to whistle, hands clasped behind her back, as she trudged the highways and byways—mostly byways—of her division after darkness had fallen. This was making virtue of necessity, for it was essential to make some kind of noise to scare off the wild creatures that lurked in the undergrowth along the sides of the road. However, there was always one point at which she could burst into song—where the tune 'Mariners' was incorporated into the march, with which there were associated the lines of Hugh Bourne and William Sanders:

> Grace is flowing like a river,
>   Millions there have been supplied;
> Still it flows as fresh as ever
>   From the Saviour's wounded side;
>   None need perish,
>   All may live for Christ hath died.

Neither William Broughton, the composer, on the west coast of the United States, nor Thomas Jackson, who added his own original words, of Boston on the east coast of Britain, could ever have dreamed that one day both would have been heard in the remote interior of Sulawesi.

Seeing the evident pleasure on his visitor's face the officer suggested that she should take the machine back to the divisional home from whence it had come. So Calliss wound up this ancient piece of mechanism and put on the record. The resulting sound was scratchy enough, but to one famished listener it was like the music of the spheres. Kalawara was more than 50 miles distant but this was no more than a sabbath day's journey as she remembered that at any moment she could unstrap the machine from her horse's back and, without let or hindrance, join in singing:

> None need perish,
> All may live for Christ hath died.

Another encouraging wind of the Spirit was the obvious love which the Toraja Salvationist had for the Army flag.

Although during the Second World War the occupying power had announced that all Salvation Army signs and symbols were to be handed in—with severe penalties for any who failed to do so, many of the comrades hid their Bibles and song books, and did their best to conceal the corps flag as well. Some were secreted in tins and then buried in the ground. Others were inserted in a length of bamboo and then hidden in a wall of the house. An empty coconut shell proved another useful hidey-hole. A flag could be stitched into a cushion cover. One faithful local officer had his sewn into the lining of his trousers. Sometimes mildew or insects triumphed over these expedients, leaving the officer no alternative to crayoning the yellow, red and blue emblem on a couple of pages torn out of a school exercise book. As soon as could be arranged Australian Salvationists sent across a supply of flags—not enough for every corps, but one was given to Gimpubia in a somewhat primitive mountain area. After each Sunday's meetings the flag would be carefully folded and placed in the tin trunk which contained the corps record books and the small store of song books.

Then came the guerillas from the south. It was not long since the men of the corps had gone into the bush and, with the few hand tools they possessed, had cut and shaped sufficient timber to build a new hall. Now it was a charred ruin and, worst of all, the tin box with the flag had disappeared. As the comrades were counting up their losses, one of their number remembered a guerilla making off into the jungle with some kind of box underneath his arm. A search was organized and, after combing the undergrowth, the tin trunk was discovered— and within the beloved flag unharmed. Greatly rejoicing the soldiers marched back to the burnt-out site, where they fastened the flag to a stick where all could see. Their flag recovered, their hall could now be rebuilt—and it was.

Similar determination, in a slightly different setting, was shown by the corps at Towulu. In a fire which had devastated much of the village the Army hall and school property had been burnt down. The forest where the best timber grew for building purposes was some distance away. The village comrades had no mechanical aids—only their axes and knives, and even after felling the trees there was the herculean task of conveying the wood from the forest to the building site.

Could the divisional office help? Much as they believed in the power which could bid the mountain be removed and cast into the midst of the sea, it was still not clear how logs could be transported.

There was an answer, however. One night there was a tropical storm of more than usual intensity, the kind of occasional storm that changes the face of the landscape. The heavens opened and thunder echoed and re-echoed for miles around. Lightning played about the mountain tops and lit up the valleys. The villagers longed for day and, as dawn broke, hurried out to discover what damage had been done. The river had burst its banks. Landslides had uprooted giant trees which had then been swept along by the flood water—to pile up in a disorderly jumble close to where the Army hall had stood. There was no need for further transport. Rebuilding began forthwith. With such soldiers who could be dismayed?

8

At the grass roots

THE visit of General Orsborn to Indonesia in 1950 coincided with an increasing recognition of the responsibilities which had been carried by Calliss since the departure of Major Mrs Poutiainen. Her appointment was changed to that of divisional secretary, which did no more than regularize all that she had already been doing. In effect, hers were the kind of duties which had fallen to the veteran *Tua Janggu* since before his internment. It is true—as has already been mentioned—that soon after his farewell the division was divided into three districts, each in the care of an experienced national officer, but correspondence with the territorial headquarters in Bandung, the well-being of the officers, the maintenance of Christian standards by the soldiery, the extension of the Army's work in central Sulawesi, the financing of that work, the accurate recording of that work, the day by day oversight of all aspects of that work, fell upon one woman's shoulders.

They were broad shoulders in more senses than one—which was just as well, for even their strength was to be tested to the limit. One thing for sure—Calliss had no time left in which to feel sorry for herself. Nor was she looking for such idle moments either. Burdens were great—but so were the opportunities, and in seeking to take advantage of the one she forgot the weight of the other. Take two examples. The Christian calendar provided one kind of opportunity; the value placed by the Army on its youth work another.

In the western world Christmas has long been an established date in the social year. Even though the profoundly spiritual significance of the season may have lost some of its hold upon the white man's world, commercial zeal is enough to maintain the secular framework of Christmas. But suppose the event had first been heard of less than a century ago? Calliss once described this situation for her fellow Australians in a Christmas issue of *The War Cry* published in the Commonwealth.

54

The people in central Sulawesi have known about Christmas for only a comparatively short time. . . . Some have not even yet heard of the Babe of Bethlehem. Christmas activities are patterned after the style of Scandinavian, Dutch or English officers who have been stationed in this land—though of course without the snow. This part of the world is almost on the equator.

I have already spent four Christmas seasons here, and will share the memories of one. No one packs a case to go on tour here. A kerosene tin or sugar bag is more suitable. Luggage has to stand up to rough usage. In mine I had to remember the need for coping with all kinds of troubles—malaria, dysentery, bites, stings and various kinds of wounds. Old magazines as presents for the village elders had to be packed, as had bobby pins, pictures and pencils for the children I would meet.

The first stage of the journey was made by bullock cart at a speed of four miles an hour—or less, according to temperature. My small but strong mountain pony plodded on behind; he was needed for the real climb which came later.

Nightfall found us—for I was accompanied by four girl corps cadets—in a Moslem village at the foot of a mountain where we slept in a bamboo hut set on stilts, with goats sheltering beneath. . . . We left the bullock cart here and my pony carried me as we commenced the five-mile climb. Up and up we went; the path was only 18 inches wide in many parts, with a sheer drop of hundreds of feet at the side, and down below a rushing river. Over the tops of faraway mountains we could see the sea, and then, almost at our destination, a group of children welcomed us with their flutes.

It was good to sit down in the officer's bamboo quarters and drink the usual hot black coffee. Folk had brought their gifts to welcome me—a chicken, some bananas, a half-coconut shell of rice. Others brought their children with their skin diseases, or told me of their own troubles. I was glad to unroll my grass mat and sleep as soon as it was dark, for the day had been a long one.

I was dreaming of Australia when I was awakened by the beating of a home-made drum—a hollow log with a goat skin stretched across one end, used to call attenders to the meetings. It was cold and dark but no one in the village possessed a time piece; the people went by the sound of crowing roosters. That morning the roosters could have made a mistake—but there was no denying the drum call, so I prepared myself for the meeting.

Soon the officer came for me and we set off in the dark for the hall. Even the hall was in blackness but one could sense that a crowd was present. I knew there was to be some kind of drama for my girls were dressed as shepherds and, as they were singing, the 'Light Tree' was lit and the candles revealed about 400 Toraja faces set amid the decorations of palm leaves and orchids. Thirty years ago these people belonged to one of the most notorious tribes of head hunters. Now they were worshipping Christ, the Light of the World. . . .

The dawn was just breaking as we left the hall. . . . Next day the 'Light Tree' became a 'Gift Tree'—the first that many of the children had ever seen, and in a practical way they learnt the other great lesson of Christmas—that happiness comes in giving rather than in getting.

By contrast the district rally at Morui was a Third World illustration of General Orsborn's dictum that 'the Army marches on the feet of its youth'.

The officer in charge of this area was Major Rungka—himself one of the outstanding Toraja leaders of his day—who, under God, owed both his conversion and his subsequent opportunities for Christian service to the Army. While the First World War was still raging the then Adjutant Woodward had pioneered the work of the Army in Kantewu. Among his earliest converts was a lad who later became the first Toraja officer to hold the rank of Major, and the local arrangements for this long weekend of meetings were in his hands. Calliss herself made the journey by stages—first to Kulawi, then another day's journey to Gimpu, and thence to Morui where on the Friday the first of the visitors began to arrive. About 400 of the total number were young people—the lads in their shorts and singlets with their inconspicuous but essential knife at their waist; the girls wearing a blouse and their customary three-tiered skirt of bark cloth. Their Salvation Army uniform, song book and Bible were wrapped in a neat bundle or slung from a long pole. Those who came from such a distance that they had to camp overnight on the way also carried their ration of rice and their iron cooking pot.

The traditional Toraja hospitality eased the problem of accommodation. Some of the villagers vacated their own homes so that room might be made for the visitors. The catering was also well organized. Each of Morui's 38 families prepared rice for 20 guests twice a day. In addition the village women made ready such customary items as the favourite 'sauce' of chilli, onion and tomato, while cooking fires were kindled in the grounds of the local day school—another Army contribution to the well-being of the community. Nor did the actual meal service fall below standard, for selected villagers—so reported the Australian *War Cry* which carried an account of the event—dressed in their best clothes, marched in orderly procession, carrying the food to their guests in halves of coconut shells.

What made this weekend so unique was that it was unashamedly Christian in an area which for generations had been wholly animist and where Islam was—and still is—a faith to be reckoned with. But Calliss set the tone of the proceedings with her keynote song: 'Jesus, my Jesus'—a theme which was taken up by flute bands, string bands and singing companies, not to mention the innumerable home-made guitars which accompanied youthful voices which seemed to rest not day nor night.

Like some musical festivals in other parts of the Salvation Army world the Saturday evening programme was a lengthy one. No corps could be omitted—even though its representation was small. In that case, the more reason for it to be both seen and heard. Small was significant—and often surprising. Of every song every line had to be sung. Who or where was that self-appointed judge or divider among men who dared to say that any verse could be omitted without grievous loss? Nor did the dramatizations of selected Bible stories lose anything in their presentation. The lily looked better for gilding.

But no one wearied of the meetings or was wearied by them. As sunrise began to colour the mountain peaks the following morning the teenagers gathered for prayer. At eight o'clock there was a Scripture story for the very young, and at 10 o'clock a gathering for the elderly— each led by a Toraja officer. meantime Calliss returned to the love which had been her life in the three Australian divisions where she had been youth secretary—the folk between the ages of 13 and 25, nearly 400 all told. Again the theme song was heard, and again the One who was the Word made flesh was acknowledged not only as a figure in past history but as a living and present Saviour. It is noteworthy that these special gatherings for young people had been commenced in England by the Army's second General towards the close of the 19th century. Here was the same principle adapted—with equally happy results—to the mid-Pacific world half-way through the 20th century.

Calliss was overjoyed with the day—as was Major Rungka. In faith believing he had removed the front of the school building—an easier proposition when the material involved was bamboo instead of brick—allowing for a further 26 rows to be added to the seating. Even that was not enough to house the assembled congregation which spilled over on to the surrounding ground outside.

In the tropics little happens by halves—and in the early evening there was a rainstorm of such severity as to make a night meeting impossible. But with that organizational flexibility which increases in direct proportion to the remoteness of high authority, the meeting was simply postponed—to the following morning. No one was rushing for a train. True that Calliss had originally planned to leave early on the Monday morning. She had a long trek before her—much of it over bridle paths which had been reduced to liquid mud. But here was a waiting congregation and the weather mended its behaviour—for the time being. The best wine was kept to the last.

In the morning Major Rungka presented his 80-strong choir of men and women who, though illiterate, sang the Founder's song—'O boundless salvation'—in Oema, a local dialect. Their academic limitations proved no barrier to their personal enjoyment of the experience of which they sang. New recruits were welcomed, 14 new soldiers were sworn-in under the flag, and along with them were enrolled nine junior soldiers. Calliss had earlier dedicated 16 babies. Each child had to be prayed over individually. A general prayer for one and all would not have been enough. So Calliss had made it her practice first to speak to the parents as a group about their personal responsibility to bring up their child in the nurture and admonition of the Lord. Then she would work her way along the line, listening to each parent's pledge so to do, and then naming the child as she offered prayer for that particular one. Sometimes she was even asked to choose the name, which resulted in a hurried consultation as to what Christian names were not in general circulation in the village. At such times the Bible was always a present help.

Best of all, a number of seekers made a public confession of faith in Jesus as Saviour and Lord—one of them being a former head-hunter, a senior member of the community and consequently revered on account of his age. The whole meeting was deeply moved at the sight of this old man deliberately renouncing his traditional life-style.

All these welcome events delayed the departure of Calliss still further. Nor could she hurry to make up for lost time for she had promised to accompany an officer-mother and her three boys down to the plains. The two elder lads were put on the back of the sturdy Gamla, the mother carried the youngest on her back, and the procession started off in single file with Calliss bringing up the rear.

To the travellers' dismay another heavy rainstorm broke over their heads. Calliss had sent her own young helpers on ahead with her personal luggage, so she lacked any change of clothing nor did she even have her mosquito net with her. There was nothing to do but to improvise some kind of shelter and, with the resourcefulness of those who lack the benefits of gas or electricity, somehow conjure up a hot drink. For Calliss this misadventure resulted in recurring attacks of malaria. What she did not know at the time was that these three boys would eventually become Salvation Army officers. But these bouts of malaria would be her thorn in the flesh. Her sturdy physique was further weakend by the diet to which she was reduced, which in turn made her less able to meet the constant demands of her work upon her bodily strength. But one welcome break as 1951 was drawing to a close was the news that Senior-Captain Enid Lee was to be appointed to the clinic at Kulawi.

These two had both belonged to the famous Faith Session in Melbourne but, after commissioning, their ways had parted. While Calliss was working in Western Australia, Enid Lee had first trained, and then served, as a nurse in Queensland and New South Wales. She had long known a call to serve in China but, with the political changes taking place in the country at the close of the Second World War, that opportunity seemed to be receding. Indeed, the official reply to her offer of service read: 'We are not sending any officers to China'.

Not long afterwards a letter reached her in a handwriting which she did not recognize. It was signed 'Gladys Calliss'. What could Calliss want with her? They had been session mates but otherwise they had never exchanged so much as a Christmas card. But the young officer-nurse read:

> I have just arrived in the East Indies. I am sitting on a verandah on my way to an appointment in the central Celebes. I have an overwhelming urge to write and ask you if you would consider working in the Indies as many of the patients in our hospitals here are Chinese. Was your call to China or to the Chinese?

The upshot was that after an introductory spell at the maternity clinic at Makasar, and a longer term at the William Booth Hospital at Surabaya, Enid Lee could have been seen with Gladys Calliss riding away on the wooden seat of a 'bendi'—a horse-drawn open cart—from the harbour at Donggala. The 16 years since their joint commissioning were covered by a flood of eager conversation as the two Australians renewed their past fellowship an ocean's distance from their own homeland.

Calliss took Enid Lee first to her own divisional headquarters at Kalawara and then, after a night's rest, shared the journey—uphill and on foot—to Kulawi. Three days later she accompanied her one-time fellow cadet on a preliminary tour of the area which the clinic served. No necessity to point out the need for qualified help to one who herself was a qualified nurse. Even the homely remedies which Calliss took round with her had been regarded by some as a species of beneficent magic. She had followed Woodward's practice of painting with iodine the huge goitres which afflicted some poor souls and, when she knew not what to prescribe, there was always an aspirin and a prayer—a treatment which had been known to effect the needed cure, at least in the mind of the patient. Doubtless this is heresy in Harley Street, but then there was nobody from Harley Street in Sulawesi.

But Enid Lee was; she would be an angel of mercy who, by way of return, might welcome simple instruction in the culinary practices of the Toraja countryside. Most domestic chores would be undertaken by the three Toraja girls whom Enid Lee found awaiting her at the clinic. Calliss had enjoyed similar assistance, for there were always lads and girls from villages in the interior who were eager to learn from such service with western officers. This arrangement was a two-way benefit—to the officers themselves and to the young folk who were thus introduced to the wider world which lay beyond their Pacific island.

Calliss could stay only a matter of days at Kulawi. She would have wished to remain longer with Enid Lee. It was good to be able to hold a conversation in English once more, but the office at Kalawari was calling. Its facts and files and figures had still to be tackled by one pair of hands—though relief was in the offing for in August 1952, Captain Melva Trembath arrived at Kalawara. None too soon either, for early in 1953 Calliss was transferred to Bandung where she was given a less exacting appointment in the trade department on the territorial headquarters so that her strength might be built up for her return to Australia on homeland furlough in time for Christmas.

The work in Sulawesi did not suffer, however, for fresh reinforcements brought the divisional staff up to full strength. And Calliss felt her spirit refreshed and her physical strength renewed as she shared Christmas with her family and friends. By the middle of 1954 she was ready for duty again and rarin' to go.

9

Inside Kramat Raya 55

ON her return to Indonesia in June 1954, Calliss was appointed in charge of the women's side (or section) of the Army's training college for officers in Jakarta. Though she could not have known it at the time, this was to be a watershed in her life. The city, already hovering on the three million mark, was to be her base for the next 11 years spent in preparing Indonesian young men and women for their life's vocation.

Ended now was the trudging by night over country tracks; the cover of an improvised road shelter when overtaken by a tropical storm; the solitary wrestling by the light of an oil lamp with books of account and official returns; the communing with one's own spirit because there was not always someone else of one's own race or tongue with whom to commune. Now her 'marching orders'—the name given to word of a new posting—plunged her into the life of the principal city of the recently-constituted republic which, if fully extended elsewhere on the map of the world, would stretch from Manhattan Island in the west to beyond Timbuktu in the east.

Jakarta itself was no mean city. Here met east and west, past and present. Modern skyscrapers overlooked shanty town areas. Newly-constructed highways bestraddled ancient waterways. The *becak*—a man-propelled tricycle where the passenger sat in front of the driver—competed for custom with the western automobile. Street traders hawked their goods in front of departmental stores. Breweries and tanneries stood cheek by jowl with university and scientific institutions. The call of the muezzin was the most insistent sound in the city, for the inhabitants—like their fellows in the countryside—were 90 per cent Moslem. Buddhists, Hindus and Christians were also rans statistically. Salvationists do not claim that minorities are always right but they have long learned from their Lord of the power of the mustard seed and the leaven. They have proved—*pace* Voltaire—that God is not always for the big battalions. They had need of this faith, for the sea of Indonesian life was still heaving uncertainly, often

61

angrily, in the wake of the events which led to the acceptance by Mohammed Hatta on the Dam Square in Amsterdam, on 27 December 1949, of the freedom of his country. Amid these unpredictable storms believers could cling only to their faith that Jesus was in the boat with them. If it had not been the Lord who was on their side, then had the waters overwhelmed them.

This new appointment marked a major change for Calliss personally. At Kalawara she had enjoyed considerable liberty of action—within the recognized administrative framework. Though she was never gazetted as other than the divisional secretary, for a considerable part of the time she was the only expatriate leader in the area and, while encouraging the district leaders to carry their full responsibilities, enjoyed freedom to exercise her own energy and initiative to further the Army's mission. Now she was part of a team. Hers was an important part—to begin with, the training of the women cadets, but there was an established pattern of training and the principal was herself an officer 10 years her senior in service who had worked in the territory since 1928. With other overseas officers the principal had seen her country and its allies surrender within three weeks of the fall of Singapore. Only missionary officers carrying neutral passports escaped arrest. With two other women officers Melattie Brouwer was imprisoned in Bandung in a cell measuring 10 feet by 12, and then interned in three different camps, conditions becoming worse with each successive move. On her release in 1945 she made her solitary way back to Bandung where, at no small personal risk and amid a three-way confrontation of the Indonesian, Dutch and British authorities, she sought to safeguard the interests—material and spiritual—of the Army. 'I will ever be grateful', wrote Calliss, 'for her influence on my life.'

The training of Salvation Army officers in what had been the Dutch East Indies was immensely aided by the opening of the Bramwell Booth memorial buildings in Bandung in September 1930. To add to the significance of the occasion a group of four men cadets arrived from mid-Celebes, accompanied by their divisional commander, the then Major Woodward. They were not the first Toraja cadets to be trained; that development went back to 1923, and each of the six training sessions in Bandung from the opening of the college until the occupation of the country in 1942 had been enriched by a quota from the Celebes. In the final year the cadets had to be hastily commissioned and later two of them were arrested by the occupying power. However they were subsequently released and made their own way along the northern coast of Java to Surabaya where they fell in with two others of their session and jointly committed themselves to an open boat hoping to regain their homeland. They braved the Java Sea but landed at Makasar. There—and truth can leave fiction standing—a Japanese naval officer who himself had been a Salvation Army cadet in Bandung in 1923, arranged for them to have the use of a small prow in which they hugged the coast until they arrived at Palu.

The next training session—fitly called in Indonesian the Peace Bringers—did not open until August 1949 (see page 32). This had to start completely from scratch. The curriculum had to be compiled afresh. Textbooks were non-existent in the mid-Celebes. As has so often happened in Salvation Army history, improvisation was the order of the day. Major Brouwer crossed over from Java to give this restart the benefit of her experience. Officers drew on the memories of their own training to help compile teaching material. Overseas officers who still carried with them textbooks from their various national training colleges translated as much as was thought relevant into Bahasa Indonesia. A Bible or a Salvation Army song book was worth its weight in gold. This Herculean task was resumed in Jakarta in 1950 when training recommenced in the building which Calliss herself had helped to clean out while on her way to her first appointment (see page 23).

But she had not long joined the training staff when the very life of this revived project was threatened. Kramat 55 was a rented property—and knocking on the door came a prospective buyer who was so certain of himself that he assured the training principal that, in his view, all that remained to be done to purchase the building was the completion of the customary legal formalities. This was news to her— but she had not endured the proscription of The Salvation Army at the hands of the occupying power to surrender her precious training college to a strange man.

Commanding Calliss and the cadets to give themselves to prayer, she hailed a *becak* and set off for Parliament house. One of the sitting members was a Christian lawyer who might be a present help in this trouble. But the buildings were closed, though the principal found a side door open and a solitary janitor in attendance. He thought that there might be perhaps one member still around—but one was enough, especially when it was the very one whose assistance was so urgently desired. The principal was sufficiently versed in the gospel to know that the importunate woman has her place in the economy of God—and once again, as in the past and without the least doubt in the future as well, wisdom was justified of her children. The Army won the right to purchase the property which it occupied, though he would be overbold who would say whether faith or works played the larger part in this deliverance from the snare laid by Mammon.

When Calliss herself became training principal she found that she was responsible for one of the three Army corps in Jakarta, and for this had the help of an additional Indonesian officer. Though it had never been easy to induce people to attend the meetings a breakthrough occurred when two or three of those interested in the youth activities of the corps persuaded some of their elders to come to the hall with them. One such was Lianna who brought first her sister and then her mother to the meetings.

Though Mrs Ang was illiterate she possessed, like many other Chinese women, a good deal of native sense. She had built up a small business by cooking and selling rice cakes until one day a fire swept through the densely crowded area where she lived, feeding on what it consumed. The flames reached the street where Mrs Ang lived, and her neighbours had almost given up hope of saving their homes when Mrs Ang stood at her door and called out: 'Let me ask my God to help us. Maybe He will save our homes.' He did! It could have been that the wind dropped, or changed direction, or that the width of the lane proved a natural firebreak. No matter! To Mrs Ang and her neighbours this was an act of God and the God who stayed the fire would be their God. And to demonstrate that this was no superstitious reaction they determined, as grace should be given them, to display those fruits of the Spirit which would make plain the reality of their fellowship with Him whom they had accepted as Saviour and Lord.

Life was hard for many of these families. They were Chinese—and that was enough for them to be objects of suspicion both to their neighbours and to the authorities. But beyond all question they were plainly Christian even to the point of being misunderstood—as when Calliss saw one of the elderly Chinese women soldiers moving up and down the aisle during the prayer meeting and apparently directing various people to the Mercy Seat. After the benediction Calliss felt she had to warn against any such excess of zeal. It would be wiser to allow would-be seekers to make up their own mind on so delicate a matter. To which the reply was that those who had gone forward had already been given sufficient instruction concerning the Christian faith for them to know what they were doing. The significance of their final act of committal had been fully explained to them.

With such soldiers in her corps Calliss had little difficulty in putting into operation what—in the Army's earlier days—had been known as the ward system. For the purpose of practical evangelism the area in which the corps operated was divided into districts (or wards). An experienced local officer (a lay man or lay woman) was placed in charge of each section and was in turn assisted by a number of soldiers. In this way the entire strength of the corps was mobilized to care and share.

However, the main concern of the principal continued to be the training of the cadets for it is undeniably true the world over that the Army's success depends upon the quality and dedication of its officers. In the Third World this means the quality and dedication of its indigenous officers. It could have been that in the old colonial days the paternalistic qualities of the civil administration were reflected—albeit unwittingly—in the structure of Christian missions. Signs that this approach was already being found wanting were highlighted in a report by the territorial commander, Lieut.-Commissioner Arend Beekhuis, immediately prior to Pearl Harbour. There were four expatriate officers in the Netherlands Indies to every three national and, more seriously still, though the Army had already been at work in the colony for 48 years, only two married couples among the indigenous officers had as yet attained the rank of Major. Over the next 40 years the situation was to change out of all recognition. Of today's roll of 396 active officers and cadets, only 22 (at the time of writing) are expatriates. In this radical shift which brought an Indonesian to the leadership of the Army's work in the Republic first in 1965, and again in 1980, the training college played a significant part in the all round development of the officer corps.

To say that the hour and the woman met when Calliss was appointed training principal is not to reflect upon her dedicated predecessor nor her gifted successors. She was then in her early 40s and her physical energies had recovered from the demands of her service in Sulawesi. One Salvationist reporter from International Headquarters who visited Indonesia at this time described her as possessing 'the intensity of a human dynamo'.

Her command of the language could rarely be faulted. The writer was in her company when paying his respects to President Sukarno, and the conversation became so free and animated that he broke in to ask how long Calliss had been in the country. 'Exactly 20 years' was her reply—which the President countered by observing that it was high time she took out an Indonesian passport. This was a hard saying—but the answer was that a Salvationist had no other aim but to serve the people around him without regard for the nature of his own passport—or theirs. Calliss had voluntarily made Indonesia her second homeland, and so it was to be for a quarter of a century.

Meanwhile she sought to lift the spiritual and intellectual sights of all who entered the training college. Under God her predecessor had brought the work of training back from the dead, and in her footsteps Calliss sought to plant her own. The language question was basic. Cadets were drawn from Ambon, Bali, Timor, Sumatra and elsewhere, but no dialects or vernacular variants were allowed in class room or meeting hall. As principals, past and present, had spoken Bahasa Indonesia, the official language of the Republic, cadets could do no less. As varied as their origins, so had been their past occupations. Some were drawn from the farm or the fields; some were trained nurses, some had been qualified teachers; some had served in social institutions or in the homes of expatriate officers—but all had worked. No one was accepted who had not been employed for 12 months prior to the date of his application to enter. This was no easy option for the work-shy—though anyone who was unfortunate enough to have been unemployed but who could give proof of a genuine sense of vocation, was found work—often in an Army institution. In this practical way every candidate could demonstrate his mettle.

Educational standards were gently but persuasively raised. To six years in the lower school was added three in the junior high. A further three years in the senior high, which brought the leaving age to 18, was also encouraged. In due course the residential term in the training college itself was extended to two years. These requirements were not intended to daunt any willing spirit but just to ensure that those two indispensable partners, heart and head, were equally yoked.

Life was real and life was earnest at Kramat 55. The morning bell was rung at six o'clock. As the Army girls were later to observe in the Gowans/Larsson musical *Glory!*—

> Cleanliness is next to godliness,
> Soap and water are divine—

so the cadets waged war to the death against all tropical forms of creepies and crawlies and long-legged beasties. Every inch of every tiled floor was washed once every day. These and similar tasks attempted and accomplished, breakfast could be enjoyed with a clear conscience at seven o'clock—after which the cadets shared a period of united prayer and then gave themselves to their private devotions. Subsequently there would be a lecture by the principal or other appointed officer, followed by a coffee break and then classes in Bible study, Christian doctrine, Church history or Salvation Army discipline.

The midday meal was followed by a short siesta. Only mad dogs and Englishmen went out in the noonday sun. Then the programme was resumed with renewed vigour with preparation for public meetings, or guidance in Salvation Army procedures, or private study as need or interest might dictate. In conjunction with the Indonesian Red Cross first aid courses were also undertaken by men and women cadets alike. Welcome too were the regular singing practices, for one of the valued gifts of the Christian Church to the Indonesian people is the wealth of western sacred music and song. Salvationist visitors are always charmed with the mastery and quality of the songs to be heard in Army meetings. Four part harmonies possess an added dimension of delight when sung by Indonesian voices.

Classes in dressmaking were welcomed by the women cadets and the cut of their white uniforms testified to their prowess with the needle. Even the men received elementary lessons in sewing and cooking. Such do-it-yourself skills were virtually essential away from town life—and did not come amiss in the larger centres of population as well.

There is an Indonesian fable that when God was creating man He put the necessary materials into an oven and waited—too long. The end product came out black—overdone. He tried once more, but was impatient and the result came out white—underdone. The third attempt was successful—a glossy chocolate brown; what an Australian might describe as 'a lifeguard's end of season tan'! Clothe the slim figure—for few Indonesian lads or girls carry any excess weight—in a trim uniform whose appeal lies in its simplicity, and there is a figure to delight the eye and warm the heart—a happy mean between western sophistication and eastern asceticism.

Certainly cadets' training in Jakarta possessed a savour not always evident at 2130 Bayview Avenue, Toronto, 303 Royal Parade, Melbourne, or other similar establishments. There was, for example, the savour of the unexpected, which could be the unwelcome as well. A couple of instances must suffice. A lad who entered Kramat 55, while Calliss was the principal, had regularly deposited his weekly savings with his employer against the day of his arrival until these had amounted to 1,000 rupiahs. But the night before he left his home the government devalued the currency by half. His 1,000 became 500—without any possibility of redress.

A girl making her way to the training college had a 70-mile trek through rough country before she could reach a main road and find a jeep to take her to the nearest port. But there she had to wait for a month for a boat to Jakarta and, waiting, used up all her savings. There was nothing to do but to trek home again and start saving once more. The second time she made it.

Once in training there was the savour of the unfamiliar. Cadets the world over know the value of literature evangelism and the place of the ubiquitous *War Cry* in such a crusade. But how many set about such work with a call from the minaret still echoing in their ears that no Moslem should buy a Christian paper? In such a situation it is some comfort to recall that only what is effective is banned by its opponents, so the sale of the *Berita Kesalamatan* in that particular period was pursued with still greater zeal. The first three or four days in every month were given over to this task. Cadets walked miles selling the paper from door to door. When a literature crusade was planned, cadets would set up a pitch on the pavement or in the market like any other street trader. In common with every other edition of *The War Cry* the paper is printed, published and promoted by Christian people, using the language of the people to bring the Christian gospel to the people. When supplies were exhausted the same methods would be followed with Christian literature in general. Again, in the manner of any itinerant vendor, a cadet would unroll his mat and spread out his stock of gospels, Bible portions and Christian material for inspection, for discussion and—hopefully—for sale. The women cadets would mingle with shoppers of their own sex and ply their Christian wares as well. As all around there were traders galore using their undoubted skills to dispose of food and clothing and medicines and pins and needles and trinkets and sweets, there were always folk whose curiosity would bring them to a halt at the sight of the uniform of the *Bala Keselamatan*.

There was a savour of danger as well.

'What are you doing here?' asked the leader of an armed patrol on the hunt in down-town Jakarta for wanted men. His troop had quietly and expertly cordoned off a prescribed area but all their net contained was one foreign woman who spoke Indonesian fluently—in their eyes a suspicious sign; foreigners were not usually so much at home in their language unless they were up to some mischief—and 10 or a dozen young people, simply but neatly dressed. (In reality this was a small party of cadets headed by their principal, on a perfectly legitimate evangelical campaign.)

So straight a question merited a straight answer—though possibly not the kind of answer which the patrol leader was expecting. 'We are telling the people that they should live good lives, and, that instead of harming one another and stealing from one another, they should love one another. This they can do by the help of God.'

The military officer was a trifle nonplussed. The existence and omnipotence of God is the first of the five principles in the 'Pantja Sila'—the basis of the Indonesian constitution. With such a statement of intent from the cadets' campaign leader he could only concur. 'Go ahead', he said as he turned himself about. 'We need all the teaching of that kind we can get.'

10

Outside Kramat Raya 55

LIFE outside the college grounds was as strenuous as life within. This is because the end aim of every Salvation Army school for officers' training is to produce men and women whom no emergency will find wanting. This rule holds good as much in Trivandrum as in Tokyo, in Bochum as in Brazzaville. Concern for bodily needs goes hand in hand with concern for spiritual needs. Daily bread and the Living Bread are offered with equal reverence and equal readiness. Though to some of these trainee officers John Donne might not even be a name, with him they are 'involved with mankind'.

This role did not come hard to the young men and women at '55', for Salvation Army pioneers in the Netherlands colony of Java began by turning their back upon white society, choosing to live in the mountain village of Sapuran in order to identify themselves with the people. After all, love is a language which needs no translating, and when its disciples rented a house for five shillings a month, and the modest hall they built for their Christian worship was made of bamboo, measured 30 feet by 18 feet and cost less than a 10 pound note, their actions spoke louder than words. With such examples before them the cadets were not surprised by the variety of tasks which they were required to undertake. There was no mistaking the call of their training principal to add works to their faith.

Except in war time fire-fighting skills are not usually on the curriculum of a training college, but the fires which swept with un-welcome regularity through the more densely populated areas of Jakarta gave the cadets the opportunity of coping with human need in one of its most tragic forms. There were always the very old, almost so feeble as to need carrying bodily to a place of safety. There were often the very young too bewildered to know in which direction safety lay. Some were too panic stricken to be able to escape the fire. Sheer terror deprived others of the power of movement. For the cadets this was caring beyond the call of duty—until Calliss discovered that some of the official firefighters were pushing her lads and girls forward where they themselves were unwilling to go.

This was behaviour which she was not prepared to tolerate. In any case, physical fire was not the only enemy. There were fires of racial prejudice such as nearly consumed the hapless Eurasians who were summarily deported in 1957. Like those upon whom the Tower of Siloam fell they were not sinners above the rest. With other minorities at various times in various lands, they were made a scapegoat for the misdeeds of others. Many were the descendants of mixed marriages several generations earlier and neither they, nor their children, had known anything other than the tropical warmth of the mid-Pacific. Now they were to be forcibly dispatched to a chillier land which they had never seen, which itself was suffering the aftermath of hostile occupation, which was even more crowded than their own, and which had to import food in order to live. But whatever their personal anxieties as they struggled to board the transports which were to take them to a land they knew not of, they discovered a few youthful white-uniformed figures willing to help them in their plight.

Someone in this little group was always ready to hump an outsize piece of luggage up the gangway, or to take over the care of a restless crying baby, or to produce almost from nowhere a large hot black coffee, or to say a word of encouragement to some unfortunate on the verge of collapse. Someone in this stage army of the good could find their way as if by magic to the most distant cabin deep in the bowels of the ship, or discover the suitcase which had vanished from the dockside into thin air. Only there was no magic about it at all—simply service given in the name and for the sake of Him who is always concerned for those who are passing through deep waters. The names of these voluntary followers of St Christopher may be remembered only by very few but, like that of Ben Adhem, may head the list when the books are opened for their unforced willingness to help travellers in trouble.

But some of those who stayed at home went hungry also. This may seem hard to credit in a country of which it has been said: 'Poke a stick into the ground and in a couple of months you will have a tree.' The plains and hillsides look bountiful. Vegetables and fruit can grow to giant size. The eye can feast upon the contrast between the glossy slopes where the tea bushes grow and the pale green rice plants in the valley beneath. But the cost of prestige projects, together with a decline in food production, plus an increase in essential imports, resulted in more than one devaluation of the currency. Even the calls to sacrifice made by Sukarno himself failed to halt inflation. 'Add maize and sweet potato to your diet of rice', he pleaded. 'I myself eat maize at least once a week.' And how much else, was a common thought—uttered or unexpressed.

The Indonesian does not think that he has had a meal without rice. Calliss had learnt that while still in Sulawesi. She also knew what it was for the food stores at Kramat Raya 55 to be virtually empty, though there were those who thought that her reserves were boundless and, asking of her, fully expected to receive.

There were countries, churches and societies that helped generously—Church World Service, Oxfam, CORSO†, World Vision Inc., Help the Aged, Inter-Church Aid, Bread for Brethren††, various Red Cross Societies, numerous women's and youth groups attached to The Salvation Army, SIMAVI*, not to mention a multitude of private donors in east and west alike. Happily The Salvation Army in Indonesia has long been a member of the National Christian Council and so is accepted as one of the most reliable of relief agencies in the Republic. Over many years milk, bread, cooking oil, grains, vitamin tablets, beans and sometimes tins of meat have been distributed over a wide area to families where need was the greatest, though there must have been times—the early 1960s was one such period—when Calliss must have felt herself cast in the role of the widow of Zarephath with but a handful of meal left in a solitary barrel.

One day there were but five kilograms of rice left in the training college store—not even enough for the cadets' food on the morrow. That afternoon a mother came to the door pleading that she had nothing to give her children for their evening meal. Of her want Calliss answered her plea, and a grateful woman left with the immediate needs of her family supplied. As was their custom the training college staff and cadets made known their needs to the Lord in prayer. Experience had taught them to trust in Him, and there was a sense in which they felt sorry for those who always had enough and to spare. They were deprived of that inner confidence possessed by those who believe that, despite all appearances to the contrary, their wants were known to Him who had chosen them for His own.

Within hours there was a call from the food distribution officer on

† The New Zealand Council of Organizations for Relief Service Overseas.
†† Relief department of a Swiss inter-church federation.
*A private Dutch organization, centred in Haarlem, working under the device: *Succurens in mundo afflictis viribus iunctis.*

72

the National Christian Council. Had the training college any space to spare in its store rooms? Was there any space? The speaker must have been joking! He was not! There were five tons of rice to be delivered and the trucks would start unloading first thing in the morning. The cadets' prayers were changed to praise—not merely on their own account but because the immediate needs of thousands of families—Moslem, Buddhist and Christian alike—could now be met.

At another time coffee became both scarce and expensive. To have to go without coffee is as much a deprivation to the Indonesian as having to go without rice. Then a telephone call from the harbour authorities announced that some bags of rice had fallen from a crane and burst open on the dockside. If the Army would like to clean up this disaster area they could have it for free. Calliss knew what to do with the sweepings. Rice had to be washed and cleaned anyway before it was cooked—so off went an officer and a group of cadets to the docks.

When the working party arrived they found that the contents of a couple of bags of best export coffee beans had also split open and their contents were mixed up with the other general litter. The first task was to sweep the dockside clean; the second to bring home the spoils; the third to separate the coffee beans and the rice from the general refuse. Willing hands set to work. The rice was cleaned, washed and made ready for distribution. Then the coffee beans were washed, dried, roasted and ground and, as the labourer is always worthy of his hire, the officers and cadets drank their own health for once in a quality coffee which they could never have afforded in the shops.

Sometimes the training college entertained angels unawares though, as the Scripture teaches, not all angels always look the part. Overseas embassies would ask help for one of their nationals stranded in Jakarta through a plane delay or some financial embarrassment. At that time there was little accommodation available in the city between the plushiest of hotels and the seediest of lodging houses. On one occasion the college sheltered a group of German hitchhikers; on another a ballet dancer awaiting the arrival of a delayed liner; on yet another an Australian Mick who could not bear to be idle and so paid for his keep by painting every door and wall in the place which, in his judgement, seemed to stand in need of freshening up. Mick preferred to have his meals with the cadets, and before long found himself in earnest conversation with one of the young Indonesian men officers. There were questionings as to what fruit, if any, these conversations might bear, but a year or more later a Salvation Army officer in the outback in the Northern Territory was surprised to be handed a five pound note—a substantial contribution in pre-inflation days—to be sent with his warmest greetings to the training college in Jakarta.

On yet another occasion an Australian couple telephoned from one of the international hotels in the city to say that they were on their way home after sharing in one of Dr Billy Graham's crusades in Manila. They did not feel at ease, however, at having to spend what they described as 'the Lord's money' on their own comfort in a luxury hotel. Could the training college take them in? A cynic might dismiss this as a disingenuous method of securing cheap hospitality. But having been entertained at the college and having seen the cadets at work, this husband and wife—on returning home—arranged for the purchase of a Holden van for the Army's services in Jakarta. Bread cast upon the waters indeed!

There could have been two reasons for this generous gift—the first, the obvious needs which could not be hid and, the second, the manifest dedication of the cadets to the task of meeting those needs. Each training session concludes with what is called—in Salvation Army parlance—a covenant day, when cadets make a voluntary pledge of lifelong service as officers of The Salvation Army. This is not infrequently an emotional occasion but on this particular day Calliss was startled to see a young cadet advancing to the Mercy Seat with a broad smile upon his face—for which reason Calliss subsequently took him privately to task.

'But Brigadier,' he protested, 'what would you have me do? This is truly the happiest day in my life. It has always been my desire that God should have all there is of me—like our Founder said about his own life. I have wanted to do this since I was a boy, and now that I have signed my covenant how can I be other than happy?' The one-time cadet is fulfilling his calling as happily now (at the time of writing) as then.

One of the most mixed-up journeys which Calliss undertook during her term as training principal was her voyage to Sulawesi in order to conduct a refresher course for officers stationed in her old division. In anticipation no proposal could have been more welcome—especially as the journey was to take place immediately after a commissioning so that she might travel with a group of officers newly appointed to serve in their own homeland.

But transport conditions were still chaotic and, on the ship loaned by the Japanese Government for inter-island traffic, the best bookings available consisted of one third-class berth for Calliss and fourth-class deck space for the rest of the party. With forebodings which were to be more than justified Calliss found her bunk in an outsize open dormitory occupied by more than 100 servicemen together with some of their wives. Her berth—save the mark—was the topmost of a group of four, with fellow travellers alongside and below her, separated by a wooden plank little more than six inches high. As she seemed to be the only white woman in the entire room she hardly stayed to excuse herself but returned with haste to the fourth class deck space. There she added her personal belongings to a laager-like barrier of luggage where, with her comrades, she lived, ate and slept for the next eight days and nights. Lest anyone think of this as an unconventional yet nevertheless acceptable mode of travel, let it be added that if this area of the deck was just above the water line, it was also immediately over the engine room.

To leave one's patch undefended was to risk losing it, so a rota was established by which the young men officers rose at four o'clock in the morning—two to fill the party kettles with boiling water for coffee and two to fill the party buckets for the equally essential task of washing behind the cover of strategically arranged sheets. The appointed bathrooms were virtually unusable with the drains choked and consequently the floors awash. Then the duty rota would line up again for the rations—usually cold rice with a green vegetable cooked in coconut milk, together with half a salted duck egg or a piece of salt fish. At Makasar there was a blessed break—which meant a proper bath at the Army's maternity clinic in the town and a civilized meal. Then back to the *Koan Maru,* clambering over the still loftier mountain of cargo and baggage taken aboard at the port. If not cabin'd, Calliss and her comrades found themselves still more closely cribb'd and confin'd. But in this unhelpful setting they sought to witness to their faith by singing Christian songs, reading the Bible and offering daily prayer.

The next dismaying fact was that the ship was not going to call at the immediate port of disembarkation but would first sail on to Manado at the most north-westerly tip of Sulawesi, putting in at Donggala only on the return journey. Nor was Calliss put any more at her ease by the announcement that all foreigners must report to the immigration authorities on arrival. Her police permit was made out for central Sulawesi only and here was she, through no fault of her own, in another part of the island altogether.

As at Makasar there was more scrambling over baggage and cargo, then down the ship's ladder into a waiting canoe, then still more clambering over rows of small boats moored to the dockside, and so on to the immigration offices. At that moment Calliss could have wholeheartedly challenged Robert Louis Stevenson's dictum that to travel hopefully was a better thing than to arrive. Mercifully she was asked for only a nominal 50 rupiahs, in exchange for which her identification card was given another stamp. An unexpected—and therefore all the more welcome—bonus was a dish of fish, deliciously cooked by the officer's wife, to be taken back to those still on board. Laden with some fresh fruit as well, Calliss renegotiated the lines of small boats fastened to the dockside, found a place in the waiting canoe, once more climbed the ship's ladder and regained the fourth deck—only to find that her comrades were barely holding their embattled line against the invasion of further newcomers. The claim made by some of these that possession constituted nine points of the law had to be contested—albeit without bitterness, for Donggala would be in sight on the morrow.

The remaining cause for concern was whether their comrade Salvationists would be at Donggala to greet them. After all, they had been expected at least three days earlier—and Kulawi, the divisional centre, was 50 miles up country. Again prayer was offered—and again prayer was answered, for God helps His children to use their brains. As their vessel turned inshore the sorely tried company of Salvationists saw a barge pulling towards them with the divisional commander waving an ecstatic welcome. The belated arrivals answered with their special biblical cheer which in English is spelt 'H-a-l-l-e-l-u-j-a-h'. In the previous week scores of cockroaches had met an untimely end—the delicately nurtured among readers may wish to refer to this species of orthopterous insect as the *stylopyga orientalis*. The casualty rate among bed bugs—again for the refined the *cimex lectularius*—had been equally heavy, though this still left an even larger number of lice to be dealt with as soon as hot water and disinfectant were available in sufficient quantities. In her diary Calliss recorded that the journey along the unlit uphill road to Kulawi was something of a nightmare—but it was blessedly cool and a blanket at night was a welcome luxury.

The response to the refresher course was ample recompense for the hazards of the journey—and for good measure there were youth councils, weddings, dedications and swearing-in of new soldiers as well. Local officers and soldiers were radiantly happy to see their former leader again. Their simple gifts of food and fruit bespoke their joy, and Calliss herself was equally enheartened to see how many of them were standing fast in their faith. The voyage back to Jakarta was

76

less tiresome, and life at the training college, where all was as clean as the most scrupulous could desire, and as well ordered as the most methodical could plan, was doubly appreciated after 48 days' absence.

A refresher course for Calliss herself was more welcome still as she found herself appointed a delegate to the International College for Officers in London for the July/September, 1962 term.

This was the 30th session of the brain-child of General Albert Orsborn. Each consisted of 24 officers, men and women, single as well as married, who met in a property specially acquired for this purpose on Sydenham Hill, South London. Approximately four sessions were held each year. The subjects handled, and the lecturers taking part, were as varied as the countries from which the delegates were drawn. No more stimulating experience—both spiritually and intellectually—could befall any officer, especially with the General (in this instance Wilfred Kitching) and the Chief of the Staff (Commissioner Erik Wickberg) taking a personal interest in this unique company who, in most instances, had never met one another before even though all were engaged in the same calling. But though relishing to the full the delights of this fellowship, Calliss did not forget those whom she had left behind her. She spent only a limited amount of her free time in sightseeing, but used most of her personal money to send back to Jakarta items rarely seen in the shops there or, when they were available, were prohibitively priced. So such items as dusters and dishcloths, cheese and chocolate were regularly posted to, and gratefully received by, comrade officers in Indonesia.

It was well for her that she had been given this opportunity for personal contact with the Army's international leaders, for in Jakarta coming events were already casting their heavy shadows before. Arson began to ravage parts of the city—at one time so close to the training college that the men cadets had to carry their possessions from their dormitory to a place of safety. But the college itself suffered no damage so that the cadets were able to provide food parcels for those who had lost their home in the flames.

Soon the British colony itself was attacked. Truckloads of chanting young men drove along the Kramat Raya and Calliss, watching them go by, could only wonder where the next outbreak of mindless violence would be. She was sad because she had made Indonesia her second homeland. She had lived among its people long enough to care for them. In their right mind none were more kind or more courteous. But she had not long to wait. Within the hour smoke was rising from the nearby British Embassy. The expatriate families who lived in the neighbourhood suffered as well for the demonstrators carried their furniture—and even their children's toys—out on to the street and set everything on fire in front of the very homes which had been ransacked. The next day the British women and children left, as did the Australian—and there was a strong suggestion that all the overseas Salvation Army women officers should leave the country as well. But it was not followed up—and Calliss and her comrades were to live through the abortive coup of October 1965, which ultimately led to Sukarno's resignation from the presidency some 18 months later.

More significant for The Salvation Army was the hint that an overseas leader was neither acceptable as the territorial head nor as the principal of the training college. How could anyone not born and bred an Indonesian truly understand the needs and aspirations of the Indonesian people? The answer is that many a Christian leader has been a Jew to the Jews and a Greek to the Greeks, though it is not easy for a nationalist government, struggling against odds to establish their country's identity in a post-colonial age, to understand such a New Testament stance. But with wisdom the Army's international leadership acted quickly. The Australian territorial commander was farewelled, and fortunately the right man to succeed him was close at hand. Since 1960 the second in command in Bandung had been Jacobus Corputty, son of the Regent of Rumohkai on the island of Ceram. He had been a Salvation Army officer since 1937, and had twice refused to resign in order to assume the regency. He was appointed territorial commander forthwith, and another Indonesian officer was given the post of training principal.

What then of Calliss? In her office at the training college she was making ready for her successor and awaiting word from International Headquarters as to where her next field of activity would be. She was still in her early fifties and could therefore look forward to a further period of fruitful service. As it was the holiday season she took a few days' break to prepare for whatever lay ahead. To her surprise—and yet her pleasure—she was appointed as the new second-in-command for the Indonesian territory as from 6 August 1965.

No rule so general that does not admit some exception—and Calliss was the exception which demonstrated that someone who was not an Indonesian after the flesh could nevertheless understand the Indonesian heart and serve the highest interests of the Indonesian people—as the next eight years were abundantly to prove.

78

11

Jalan Jawa 20, Bandung

THE post of chief secretary, or principal executive officer, in any Salvation Army territory calls for considerable wisdom of mind and grace of spirit—never more so than in Indonesia in the second half of 1965. For the first time an Indonesian national had been entrusted with the leadership of the Army in the Republic, and for the first time a woman—and a white woman at that—had been appointed his second. This new arrangement required no small degree of mutual understanding and acceptance, but the partnership of Corputty and Calliss—or it could equally well read Calliss and Corputty—was the right team for the right hour. Both leaders were dedicated to the spread of the Christian gospel and the progress of the Army.

Well that this was so, for within weeks the country was involved in a head on clash between two factions as unforgiving as Guelph and Ghibelline or York and Lancaster. The attempted coup in September 1965, was no slap-happy affair with the proletariat manning makeshift barricades. Plans had been carefully laid at all levels. In such a situation the Salvationist prefers to endure suffering rather than inflict it. At all times the Army's mission is to bind up the broken in heart and the wounded in body. Nevertheless as all hospitals, homes and meeting halls belonging to the *Bala Keselamatan* were usually identifiable as such it was not difficult for any so minded to wreak their wrath on those serving there. In the event, however, the attempted coup recoiled pitilessly on the heads of its instigators and, in the unrestrained bloodshed which followed, the innocent suffered with the guilty.

The recent administrative change meant that Calliss now worked from the territorial headquarters in Bandung, but on this particular Thursday she had returned to Jakarta to conduct the first Spiritual Day (a Salvation Army form of 'retreat') with the cadets who had just entered training. This she had been glad to do for, truth to tell, she had been missing her former charges at Kramat Raya 55. But when she left the following morning to take the train back to Bandung the usual road to the station, which passed the presidential palace, was sealed off by troops. The reason for this was not immediately obvious, and the fact that the train arrived on time at Bandung allayed any immediate fears. As the day wore on, however, rumours—wild and even wilder yet—began to circulate. Confusing announcements bewildered listeners to the radio, though not until 4 October—when the bodies of seven murdered generals were discovered in a well, covered with leaves and branches, about a dozen miles outside Jakarta—did the Indonesian people realize the true significance of what had euphemistically been dismissed as 'the September 30th Movement'.

Of those tragic days Callis later wrote:

The following months were very dark for Indonesia. It is said that about half a million people lost their lives. . . . Some villages lost every man they possessed and the crops were left to die. Under cover of the general disorder old scores were settled. Many hardly knew who was friend and who was foe. Some of the young folk we ourselves knew were arrested just because in the past they had associated with others who belonged to suspect organizations.

Sometimes shots would be heard, and then we would see bodies dragged along the road and flung into trucks. As we travelled from village to village in our Salvation Army uniform in the course of Salvation Army duty, we would be stopped for an inspection of our luggage and of the car in which we were travelling every few miles.

Of course any figure of lives lost was largely academic because in the minds of some of the protagonists the struggle assumed the character of a 'holy' war. The adjective is a misuse of words for it became a cover phrase for a savagery that knew no mercy whereas, by Christian standards, a single drop of blood shed unnecessarily cries from the ground. Nurses, expatriate and national, could only look on helplessly when groups of armed men burst into the theatre of a Salvation Army hospital and protest vainly when a patient was dragged from the operating table.

Even the staff themselves were frequently in danger as when, one Sunday morning, the European officer matron was driving her nurses to the corps holiness meeting. During these troubled days one of their favourite songs was Fanny Crosby's 'A wonderful Saviour is Jesus, my Lord', with the refrain:

> He hideth my soul in the cleft of the rock
> That shadows a dry, thirsty land;
> He hideth my life in the depths of His love,
> And covers me there with His hand.

This time the singing was rudely interrupted by the crackle of small arms fire. Soldiers leapt on to the road from a truck which had been preceding the hospital vehicle, and it seemed for some moments as if the nurses would be caught in a vicious crossfire.

Others had the even more disconcerting experience of finding their names on one or other of the death lists which had been prepared. Later on some were even shown the graves which had been dug in readiness for their execution. Christians were in a minority anyway—say, about eight per cent of the population—which meant that Salvationists were a minority of a minority. No one was sure whether his uniform would spell deliverance or death.

Broadly speaking, support for the coup grew from west to east of the island, and in one of the towns in the centre of Java—Surakarta, now known as Solo—a young married Lieutenant was in charge of the corps. The fiat regarding the wearing of any Salvation Army sign or symbol had already gone out, and one evening the officer returned to the town to find the railway station in hostile hands. He had previously told his people that, if they wished, they could remove their 'S's. For his part, however, if he was to die, he would die with his 'S's on. In the goodness of God, however, he was numbered among those who were hid 'in the cleft of the rock'.

Not all were so preserved from physical danger. Perhaps not everyone fully understood the implications of this evangelical faith. Perhaps some even tried to use it as a cloak for their darker designs.

In Jakarta a young man of university education professed Christian conversion and thereafter gave a good testimony. With his professional skills—he was a lecturer in law at a nearby military academy—he seemed an ideal youth leader and was so appointed, to the apparent benefit of the work. Later a united youth weekend was planned with young people from other corps participating. On the Friday evening however, as final touches were being added to the meeting preparations, the military police made an unexpected call. Skilled infiltrator or innocent victim, who knows? One thing for sure, he was never seen at the Army again. The wisest judgement for the remote spectator could be that of 'not proven', but such a verdict could be too finely balanced when passions ran high. There can be no question but that, in the confused situation, the completely innocent were sometimes falsely accused.

A Salvationist medical student was expelled from his faculty because he had been seen riding pillion with another medical student who was alleged to have been a member of a youth club suspected of Marxist leanings. Guilt by association indeed—but fortunately the Army lad had a courageous corps officer who was willing to testify that the occasional pillion ride had no political significance but was merely a convenient and speedy way home. Months of medical studies were lost, but happily the lad was finally reinstated and in due course qualified as a doctor.

In this overheated atmosphere no one was exempt from scrutiny. Calliss herself had always to have the requisite papers and permits on her person and, as a security measure, one of the government's demands was that everyone should profess a religion of one kind or another. This became the rough and ready shibboleth of the times. To lack this qualification invited condemnation as an enemy of the State. If in a spot check a man claimed to be a Moslem, he was required to recite a passage from the Koran; if a Christian, to say the Lord's Prayer. No distant observer need wax cynical over this. Even in Britain during the Second World War attendance at national days of prayer filled many a half-empty church. If immediately before the fall of France in 1940 Notre Dame was crowded with representatives from all levels of French society for a service of intercession, who can scoff at a group of mid-Javanese villagers who, when a PKI leader was killed in their district, besought the Captain of the nearest Army corps to commence meetings in their area without delay.

For some any port was good enough in a storm. It may be argued with equal justification that others were awakened to their need of a genuine faith. In the above instance the outpost thus commenced is thriving today. It would be strange if calamity did not turn some men's thoughts to God. Soldiers have been known to pray in a shell hole. And Calliss was wholly at one with her territorial leader in their joint endeavours to make sure that every convert was well and truly grounded in the faith and every officer a worthy example to the flock.

In this they had the sympathy and support of Commissioner T. H. Holbrook who had been International Secretary for Asia and Africa since 1960. In other words he was the link on International Headquarters between the General and the work of the Army on those two continents. Since 1946 the Commissioner and his wife had known the gains and pains of a missionary officer's life. While still serving in Bombay he had been asked to travel to Singapore to meet Colonel C. W. Widdowson—then in charge of the Indonesian territory—so as to secure an uncensored account of the Army's position in the Republic. The Commissioner also accompanied General and Mrs Kitching on their visit to Indonesia in 1961, and so it was not surprising that within four weeks of the assassination of the seven generals he was in Indonesia again. By this time the reaction against the attempted coup was at its height and consequently firm news was at a premium.

The chief secretary's diary for these November days records that some of the most experienced overseas officers felt that, for the sake of his own safety, their visitor should not be allowed to travel beyond Bandung. Two of them called on Calliss personally to press their point. But, to his everlasting credit, it must be said that the Commissioner insisted on travelling across Java to Semarang in the centre of the northern coastline, and then on to Surabaya in the far east—roughly the distance from London to Aberdeen. Officers there—Indonesian and European alike—had been steadfast in faith and duty and should be commended personally. Calliss accompanied the international secretary and the territorial commander and this part of her diary reads:

3 November. Left Bandung early in the morning not knowing what to expect. Many road blocks; stopped several times; car and luggage closely examined; my handbag searched and I was questioned about the presence of two fruit knives. Territorial commander explained that I was the hostess—'mother' was the word he used—and wished our visitor to enjoy the mangoes, then in season. This explanation was accepted. After many hours of travelling reached Semarang where given an enthusiastic welcome.

4 November. In Semarang for the day. Visited two institutions; meeting with officers followed by public meeting at night. Hall packed; many seekers.

5 November. Up at 4 am. Many people troubled by sight of strange star with long tail in the sky. Some older Javanese literally moaning with fear, declaring this to be a portent of great bloodshed. (Time was to prove their prophecy correct.) Again stopped many times on way to Surabaya. Luggage checked; questioned as to our intentions. Eventually reached our destination.

6 November. Air of tension everywhere. Commissioner visited institutions encouraging staff, patients and inmates. Officers' meeting in afternoon.

7 November. Four meetings today (Sunday). Interviews with officers between meetings. Many seekers. Comrades felt it to be wonderful that someone from International Headquarters should be with us at this time.

8 November. Back to Semarang; car stopped and searched five times; relief to reach hospital safely.

9 November. To Bandung. Stopped six times for inspection of papers and luggage.

10 November. Commissioner left by air for London. All of us weary after strain of travel but greatly encouraged by his presence.

The end of civil strife did not mean that there was now an interval for self-pity. Even before the firing had died away the relief work had begun. In any conflict there are those who lose whichever side wins, and among them are always wives bereft of husbands, children bereft of fathers, parents bereft of sons. In this particular situation fields had been left untilled and crops left unharvested because in village after village some obscure cultivator had been wounded, or killed, or imprisoned, or had taken with his wife and family to the roads simply in search of safety.

One illustration of the capacity of the Salvation Army officer to improvise relief services for those in need was provided at Semarang when the manager of the Bugangan colony for the homeless found himself flooded with refugees fleeing from the fighting in central Java. Makeshift huts sprang up almost overnight on the perimeter of the colony but, thanks to the generosity of Church World Service with gifts of rice and wheat, and the willing co-operation of the limited colony staff, a daily meal was provided for all. It is not surprising that these suppliers of daily bread came to be accepted by some as providers of the Bread of Life as well, though the provision of the one was never made conditional upon the acceptance of the other.

In the name of God, the compassionate, the merciful, a predominantly Moslem society also allowed Salvation Army officers to visit political prisoners—though again this privilege was never misused as an occasion for proselytizing.

As it was, it became increasingly difficult for any trouble-maker to hide his tracks. No would-be nurse could be accepted for training in any Salvation Army hospital until rigorous government screening had cleared her of involvement in the now discredited uprising. By the same official rule no one could be considered as a candidate for officership unless his loyalty to the Republic was beyond doubt. The standards for entry into training were already exacting. Reference has earlier been made to the determination shown by Calliss to maintain these. The end result was that this additional provision proved unnecessary.

So the work of strengthening any weak hands and encouraging those still fearful of heart went steadily on. In this the territory was frequently heartened by the presence and example of international visitors. In 1964 the 70th anniversary of the commencement of the Army's work in Java was marked by a visit from Lieut.-Commissioner (Dr) and Mrs A. B. Cook, leaders of the Australia Eastern Territory. The same year saw the 50th anniversary of the founding of the eye hospital at Semarang by Lieut.-Colonel (Dr) V. A. Wille, whose biography—*He Gave Sight to Hundreds*—by Lieut.-Commissioner S. C. Gauntlett was translated into Indonesian for the occasion. Another institution, the general hospital at Surabaya, celebrated its 40th anniversary at the same time—all confirming the local Salvationists in their faith that their work was well rooted in the national life.

In 1965 five Indonesian officers, representing the Javanese, Ambonese, Menadonese, Chinese and Toraja people of the Republic, travelled to London to share in the Army's international centenary celebrations, and one of them—Brigadier Pudjosumarto, the men's social secretary—was a member of the colour party that headed the processional entry into Westminster Abbey.

The year 1967 saw the Army's eighth international leader, General Frederick Coutts, accompanied by the unwearying Commissioner Theodore Holbrook, spend 14 days in Indonesia—a period which gave time not only for formal calls upon ambassadors, provincial governors and military commanders as well as for meetings in the principal centres of population, but also for unhurried consideration of some of the practical problems of the Army's work in a land so sadly weakened by internal conflict.

In the meetings Calliss was everywhere, never obtrusively but always capably—leading the prayer seasons, dealing personally with seekers and acting as an invaluable link between the visitors and her people. Highlights were many, but no one present at the final Sunday morning holiness meeting at Jakarta will forget the congress chorus, under the leadership of Major Herman Pattipeilohy (now the territorial commander) singing General Albert Orsborn's 'Peace be with thee', set to an arrangement of Handel's 'Largo in G' by Colonel A. H. Jakeway. No words could have been more relevant to the needs of a harassed people.

> Here is the good we seek,
> Message for souls distressed and hearts oppressed.
> He is of life the Lord,
> Hear ye His word . . .
> Let not your heart be troubled nor be ye afraid.

But Calliss was also there when the territorial finance council, under the presidency of the territorial commander and with their international visitors present, considered what should be done in view of the savage devaluation which overnight had reduced the value of 1,000 rupiahs to one rupiah! This was directed against currency hoarders—but, as with many such measures, hit the honest citizen hardest of all. The Salvation Army has to avoid even the appearance of evil in all its financial transactions. What then is to be done when a government decree makes a mockery of the budgeted salary scales and reduces the value of a chief secretary's allowance to a few shillings a week? Enough to say that so desperate a situation required a desperate remedy.

Nevertheless there were breaks in a clouded sky—the gift of a new Volkswagen from Oxfam for the Semarang eye hospital. A more unusual but equally appreciated gift from Scandinavia was one of 300 reams of newsprint which was used to print 10,000 copies of four Salvation Army books which had been translated into Indonesian. Much to the delight of Calliss sufficient money was also available to finance two three-day retreats where over 100 indigenous officers shared in prayer and Bible study for the deepening of their own spiritual life along with a reappraisal of the techniques of emergency relief. There has yet to be coined a word which will unite the graces of the spiritual life with the practicalities of social service and make it clear that both are rooted in a single Christian source—the charity that never faileth.

For Calliss time was marching on. She first arrived in Indonesia in 1947, was made training principal in 1957 and was appointed chief secretary in 1965. Before 1973 was out she would be retiring—but at the beginning of October 1968, she found herself in Tokyo, sharing in the first Far East Zonal Conference, led by the then Chief of the Staff, Commissioner Erik Wickberg. Here with Commissioner J. H. Swinfen and Lieut.-Colonel Gordon Barrett of International Headquarters, Commissioner Koshi Hasegawa and Lieut.-Colonel Stanley Cottrill of Japan, Lieut.-Commissioner Leslie Rusher and Colonel Chang Oon Yong of Korea, Colonel Jacobus Corputty of Indonesia, Lieut.-Colonels George Engel and Thelma Watson of Singapore, Lieut.-Colonel John Nelson and Brigadier Milton Rand of Hong Kong, and Brigadier Arne Cedervall and Major Nancy Hulett of the Philippines, she considered an agenda which ranged from the development of indigenous leadership to the place of the Brengle Institute in the Far East. Calliss revelled in this free interchange of ideas and herself read the opening paper in the session devoted to 'The selection and preparation of the missionary officer'—a subject dear to her heart.

This was but a shadow of things to come, though she knew it not. She was hoping that her final overseas furlough which would precede her retirement in Australia, might be spent in England—and expressed her hopes in writing in one of those rare personal letters which concerned herself.

International Headquarters agreed to her request and, as sometimes happens, improved on it. Furlough in England was granted—to which was added a duty tour in Scandinavia commending the cause of the missionary work which she loved so well to Salvationists who had long supported it with their gifts and their prayers. But hidden from her sight when she left Indonesia in May 1973, was the fact that an unexpected bonus of an additional four years' active service was to see more extensive travelling on Salvation Army duty than ever she had known before.

12

2 Union Place, Colombo

FOR Calliss to leave Indonesia in May 1973 was even harder than leaving Australia for the first time in July 1947. Then there had been the anticipation of a task to be attempted; now there was the inescapable sadness of a work virtually ended. But the shape of things to come suddenly changed without warning. She herself had expected nothing more than this seven weeks' series of meetings in Scandinavia, plus a happy furlough in Britain, before returning to the congenial sunshine of the land of the coolibah tree and her years of well-earned retirement. But even before she left for the first of the three European countries she was to visit, she was advised that her term of active service was to be extended. The territorial commander for Sri Lanka had unexpectedly fallen ill and, despite a speedy return to England for specialist treatment, had been promoted to Glory. Arrangements were being made to fill the vacancy temporarily, but Calliss was told that she would be assuming the leadership of the Army in Sri Lanka before the year was out.

She had never refused any appointment—not from her first commissioning to the kitchen of the training college in Melbourne. As a beginner she had turned that duty into an opportunity and now, with close on 40 years' experience behind her, she had much, much more than ever to give to the land that awaited her—and still much more to learn from it. For her the work of an officer had always meant both 'blessing and being blest'. Meanwhile her immediate mission demanded all her attention for a constant flow from Scandinavia of dedicated men and women, plus generous gifts in kind, had enriched the Army's work in Indonesia.

One of the two pioneer officer couples to arrive in Sulawesi was the Danish Charles Jensen and his wife. The first piece of literature ever to be produced in any of the native languages spoken where the Army was at work in mid-Sulawesi was a book of New Testament stories in the Idja tongue based on the gospel of Luke, the work of the Finnish

Edvard Rosenlund and published by the Dutch Bible Society. His compatriot, Heikki Juutilainen, translated the same gospel into Moma, another language spoken in Sulawesi. The Danish Wilhelm Andreas Wille who, with his wife, came to Semarang in 1907, laid the foundations of the Army's medical work in Indonesia and there remained until his promotion to Glory in 1944. During the Second World War internment by the Japanese took its toll of the expatriate officers, among whom were four from Norway, not to mention the Swedish Major J. W. Jennerstrom who was arrested and interned 'in error' in July 1942, and who, though subsequently released, died a year later.

It was therefore with a deep sense of obligation that Calliss began her tour of Norway, Sweden and Finland where, in corps after corps and in meeting after meeting, she described the four principal sections of the Army's work in Indonesia—evangelical, educational, medical and social, currently staffed for the greater part by Indonesian Salvationists themselves whom the first expatriates had trained. Some of these were the grandchildren of those who had been head-hunters in Sulawesi, and one of the smaller corps in Finland had sponsored the medical training of one such lad who now, fully qualified, was serving in the mountainous central area of his native island.

Salvationists in Sweden have never lacked in missionary zeal and, among the many who gave their lives and spent their skills for a people of other blood than their own were Nanna Roslund and Hildur Palm.

For 12 years prior to the outbreak of the Second World War Nanna Roslund had served in the small but busy hospital at Palu on the west coast of Sulawesi but the occupation of Indonesia meant the end of their work. Even when peace returned it seemed as if the lack of money and the absence of reinforcements would prevent its recommencement. Hope deferred made many a heart sick, and Calliss was serving as chief secretary of the territory when a letter bearing the Swedish postmark announced that Salvation Army bandsmen in that country were anxious to raise money for the work in Indonesia. Could a worthwhile project be suggested? So with the money raised by the bandsmen in Sweden, plus a donation from Oxfam and another from SAMAVI, a more commodious building than had ever been thought possible was erected at the fitting address of Jalan L. H. Woodward 1, to commemorate the work of Nanna Roslund and Hildur Palm.

Norway had never been slow to help either and, with the help of a generous grant from a Norwegian government agency, a brand new nurses' home was opened at the general hospital at Semarang.

The tour over, there was little time left but for Calliss to betake herself to Heathrow and leave by an overnight plane for the Bandaranaike international airport just outside Colombo. This was literally a land she knew not of and, turned 60, she was now being called upon to accept a new country, a new people, a new language and a new culture. The climate was about the same. As near as made no difference Colombo was on the same degree of latitude as Bandung. But deep in her heart Indonesia had become her second homeland. She could talk freely to the people—both in meetings and in their homes—as if she was one of them, which indeed she had become. She quickly picked up one or two conversational phrases in her new country but always in meetings, though less frequently in the office, there had to be the inevitable translator. Not that any of them were more of a hindrance than a help. Far from it. Salvationist interpreters are among the best in the world. Evangelists such as Dr Billy Graham have been glad to make use of their services. But Calliss wanted to be as close to the Sinhalese as she had been to the Indonesians. For that to come about meant that she had to care as wholeheartedly for her new countrymen as she had for her old.

This became the burden of her prayer—and the Sinhalese Salvationists responded by the warmth with which they took her to their hearts. At the airport national and expatriate comrades greeted and garlanded her in traditional fashion. To make her feel still more at home Lieut.-Commissioner Catherine Jarvis (R), who had been acting as the International Headquarters' representative since the untimely passing of Colonel William Fleming, had stayed over to preside both at the introductory officers' meeting and the public welcome at Colombo.

The new arrival was thus given time to familiarize herself with her new quarters which stood next to the Dehiwala home for girls and less than 100 paces from the fine white sandy shore and the warm welcoming waters of the Indian Ocean. It also enabled the Commissioner—the first Australian single woman officer to hold this rank—to make the acquaintance of Alice. Any domestic title would be far too inadequate a description for one who had served successive territorial commanders over many years. She may not have carried any official rank but no money would have bought the personal service given daily—virtually hourly—by the Sinhalese Alice.

This set Calliss free for the work which she had to do in Sri Lanka for she knew her time was limited. What she had to do she had to do quickly. So without delay she set out on her first objective—to meet her people. How could she lead and inspire them unless she knew them? And how could she know them unless she visited them in their towns and villages scattered over more than 25,000 square miles? North to south this pear-shaped island stretched as far as from Lancaster to Southampton and, at its broadest part from east to west, from Cambridge to Bristol. In this area lay her 48 corps and over 100 outposts, with 13 institutions and an estate thrown in for good measure. Leaving the William Booth Memorial Hall in Colombo out of the picture for the moment, for this was where the territorial headquarters was situated as well, Calliss began with the Coxhead Hall at Hewadiwela—so named after one of the Founder's most ardent helpers in Christian Mission days—and then, as speedily as possible, met her soldiers at Telampitiya, Kandy, Gambola, Mahaiyaham, Mahagoma, Helponwela, Bryanwela, Ganapinuvela, Matara, Galle, Mortumulla and Rambukanna.

But the new territorial commander had been in Sri Lanka barely a month when she had to visit the international airport once again—this time to welcome General Erik Wickberg on a three-day visit to the island. There were the inevitable garlands—planned and un-planned—with Salvationists forming a guard of honour while the Colombo Central Band played 'Joy in The Salvation Army'. There were the equally inevitable welcomes and responses after which the comrades returned with all speed to Colombo to take part in the half-night of prayer convened to ask the blessing of God upon the visit.

Happily everything ran according to plan. On the time-honoured principle of filling to the full the unforgiving minutes of any visitor's stay, the General held a well-attended press conference followed by tea with members of the local advisory board and the principal officers on the territorial headquarters. The world's press refers to working breakfasts or a working lunch. The Salvation Army has working teas—but the technique is much the same. The meal is incidental to the conversation, not the conversation to the meal.

Next morning the General met the officers in council and, in the afternoon, there was a public rally which not even the greatly increased hall seating could entirely contain. But, as is customary in any truly Army gathering, the platform was capable of accommodating the auxiliary bishop of the Roman Catholic Church, the Anglican Bishop of Colombo and the chairman of the Methodist Church. Some inkling of what the Army asks of its Generals may be gained from the fact that

General Wickberg left the same evening for further meetings in Madras.

Calliss returned to her office in Union Place which overlooked the junction of five roads. Close to the Army's headquarters and central hall was a Moslem mosque, a Buddhist temple and a Roman Catholic church. The pealing of church bells, the call to prayer by the muezzin and the sound of an Army band could each be heard at varying intervals, but the constant background to these commingled sounds was the shuffle of human feet—some hurrying to get home when the day's work was done, some dawdling because there was no home to which to go. Homeless and hungry, their harsh existence weighed heavily on the heart of Calliss. 'Give ye them to eat' was for her a word of divine command. But though she had compassion on the multitude, a few had none for her.

She had been in Colombo hardly three months when her quarters was most comprehensively burgled. Her own room was not invaded and so she slept on while the intruders carried off everything of value that could be carried off. Linen cupboards were left bare. Every electrical appliance was carefully removed. All articles of clothing, including her own best uniform—though how any fence would dispose of that is an interesting speculation—were taken away. This was breaking and entering conducted with professional expertise. A wooden shutter had been levered free, two iron bars had been wrenched from their fastenings, the fine wire mesh which covered the window had been cut away, and then well-oiled bodies had eased themselves through the opening. Silence and thoroughness were the twin hallmarks of the whole operation. Nothing taken was ever recovered.

As misfortunes never come singly, not long after Calliss fell, broke the upper part of her arm, and had to be taken to hospital. There was the customary stream of visitors, but with an unusual result. A property proposal of some local urgency had to be submitted to International Headquarters, and the territorial property board rightly felt that this could not be done without the knowledge and consent of the Commissioner. True she was in hospital, but she was receiving visitors. Could she not receive members of the property board as well? No sooner mooted than agreed. Enter the property board bearing proposals, papers and plans for the chairman's perusal. Detailed discussion ensued and a recommendation was agreed. The property board was in high feather that Salvation Army business had been dealt with so expeditiously—until they became aware of the deputy matron's disapproval. Such conduct transgressed the limits of medical propriety.

However, the Commissioner's recovery was not delayed in any way. Indeed, who can say whether her discharge was not thereby hastened? Affairs do sometimes work together for good in mysterious ways—and there were many matters outside the hospital walls demanding her urgent attention, one of them being that flood of hungry people which ebbed and flowed beneath her office window. So it was a day long to be remembered when two feeding centres were opened—one in Slave Island and the other a couple of miles distant at Rajagiriya.

By half past nine on a weekday morning a queue would begin to form, although it was not until 11.30 am that food was served when, promptly to time, a Sinhalese woman officer with her helpers would appear, bearing containers of thick nourishing soup whose sweet smelling savour carried the sure and certain promise of a meal for the hungry. By government order preaching was not allowed at any food distribution but grace could be said—and of this the Captain took full advantage. Sometimes Calliss herself wished that the grace was less lengthily didactic and more briefly devotional, but a sixth sense told the queue when to move forward—often a disused condensed milk tin in one hand while the other was extended to receive an outsize slice of freshly-baked bread. (In fairness to the service it should be said that dishes were provided but largely went unused.) Most of the beneficiaries then sat by a wall or on the edge of the gutter, dipping their bread in their soup and relishing the food as only the genuinely hungry can.

Sometimes the menu was changed to cooked rice with curried vegetables laid on a banana leaf and then made into a neat parcel. This form of food distribution was particularly suited to the rainy season when supplies could be carried to the homeless crouching in shop doorways or trying to sleep under bridges with a sack for a covering. Nor should it be forgotten that this particular work of love and mercy owed its origin to Commissioner Bramwell Tripp (R) who, when in charge of The Salvation Army in the USA Eastern Territory, set his people an example by fasting on one day each week for the benefit of the hungry in the Third World. It was this practical expression of concern which made possible this food distribution in Colombo.

But Calliss had to leave Sri Lanka for the Salvation Army's eighth High Council, though she delayed her departure until 1 May 1974. With 39 other delegates she shared in the reception given by Her

93

Majesty Queen Elizabeth the Queen Mother, in St James's Palace, and though the royal conversation with Calliss was interrupted by the unscheduled arrival of Blackie, grandmother of the royal corgies, the company was more entertained than disconcerted. Australian accents were also heard in the Westminster Central Hall when Calliss led the congregation in the responsive Scripture reading. The council's business was carried through with dispatch and, on the afternoon of 13 May the announcement was made that Commissioner Clarence Wiseman had been elected General by 29 votes out of 40. By the first Thursday in June Calliss was conducting the weekly holiness meeting in Colombo, reporting on recent events in London and thereafter resuming her round of visits to her people in Sri Lanka.

These came to be numbered among her most pleasurable experiences. The larger corps would greet their leader with all due ceremony, meeting her at the entrance to the village and after garlanding her, reading an address of welcome and presenting her with flowers, would set off in procession with drum and timbrels, with dancing girls and happy songs, to the hall where the meeting was to be held. At times fireworks would be let off without warning—until Calliss explained that, in her former appointment, an unexpected explosion of that kind would have sent her diving for cover. To spare her such indignity could she be warned in advance if the welcome proceedings were to be—'noisy' was the euphemism employed.

Sometimes there would be a 'white carpet' welcome—which meant that the visitor would be required to walk at a stately pace along a broad strip of white material, which would then be quickly rolled up, carried ahead of her, and then unrolled before she reached the end of the length on which she was walking. This could continue at times for anything up to a quarter of a mile.

The smaller villages and hamlets took Calliss into the heart of Sinhalese life. The natural beauty of the countryside would be seen in all its glory—the multi-coloured bougainvillia giving place to hibiscus and frangipani set against the immaculately kept tea plantations with tall coconut palms as a backcloth and, wherever there was a vacant space, the gentler colour of a paddy field. At any turn in the winding road might be sighted a Buddhist shrine, or a statue of the Lord Buddha himself, while groups of Buddhist monks in their saffron robes would witness by their presence that in Sri Lanka theirs was the predominant faith.

But though heavily outnumbered and with scant contact with

neighbouring comrades, the village Salvationists were nobly faithful. Often Calliss would have to leave her vehicle at the nearest road junction from which point the corps officer, armed with drum and flag, would lead his comrades in single file along the narrow ridges which separated one paddy field from another, the soldiers singing, the visitor unfamiliar with either words or music but trying to look as if she had known both from her youth upwards. Then, with the hall in sight, there would be a blessed halt while the top was cut off a king coconut and the delicately cool liquid would be poured out for her to drink, though sometimes she would be handed the coconut and invited to drink without the aid of glass or cup. She was equal to either situation and, the meeting over, there was often time to visit the sick and elderly unable to come to the hall themselves. Then there would be an unearthing of personal treasures—a faded uniform, a well-worn Bible, a photograph of some past leader. Such intimacies endeared the people to Calliss and she to them.

So with unwearying pace she criss-crossed the island, confirming her soldiers in their faith and lifting the sights of her officers. This never-ending task was greatly facilitated by the gift of the ancestral home of the first Sinhalese officer, Arnolis Weerasooriya who, within five years . of commissioning, died of cholera. If anyone is the patron saint of the Army in Sri Lanka it is—and possibly ever will be—Weerasooriya. With this gift by his family the Army in Sri Lanka acquired their first all-purpose conference centre. The property stood close to the main road south to Galle not far from the popular resort of Hikkaduwa. Within walking distance stretched the white sands which led to water so clear that the coloured fish could be seen swimming in and out of the coral reefs. After some essential adaptation and repair to the buildings, the first series of residential officers' councils were held in July 1974. This was followed up by a fellowship for the retireds and, in a territory where they numbered one-third of the total officer strength, their influence was not to be under-rated. Then followed two-day workshops for corps officers, three-day seminars for home league local officers, holiday weeks for children from the poorer parts of the capital, vacation breaks for officer-mothers and their young children, junior soldier camps, corps cadet house parties, councils for young people's local officers, as well as for selected officers—chosen across the board—who might benefit from more intensive biblical and administrative studies.

Hand in hand with these challenges to head and heart went a steady growth in practical service to the community. With the generous help of 'Bread for Brethren'—the Swiss agency concerned—a boys' training centre was opened on the Kalutara estate. Towards this home, as well as the William Fleming memorial shelter for the destitute, the World Council of Churches made liberal grants. Part of the men's industrial home in Colombo was also renovated and refurnished as an eventide home for men. The feeding programme, regularly maintained in the capital, was extended to other parts of the island as well. Thanks to the admirable 'Least Coin' project, home league members in Japan were able to provide help for mentally handicapped children in Sri Lanka.

In the midst of these many activities the territorial commander's programme included engagements in England, India and Africa—but these were so many and varied as to call for separate treatment.

13

Colombo to Colombo
via Calcutta, Dhariwal, Madras, London, Nairobi

IN her new appointment Calliss found herself the senior active Salvation Army officer in an area stretching from the Himalayas to Dundra Head and from the Indus to the Irrawaddy. Thus there fell to her the duty of representing the General at such Salvation Army functions as the retirement from active service of Lieut.-Commissioner and Mrs Fazal Masih in Calcutta. He became an officer in 1929 and, with his wife, had given almost 90 years of commissioned service between them. From there Calliss paid a flying visit to the MacRobert Hospital in the Punjab, and thence to Batala where she conducted the installation of Lieut.-Colonel Gordon Bevan as the new territorial leader.

The next inter-territorial event for her was the fourth zonal conference, held in Colombo from 13-16 January 1975, hosted by the Commissioner, presided over by Commissioner Arthur Hook, and attended by 19 of the Army's leading officers from India, Pakistan, Sri Lanka and Burma. Some of these Calliss was meeting for the first time, and all were aware of the difficulties facing any Christian movement in areas where religious differences and racial conflicts conspire to make the propagation of the gospel ha·der than ever. It is true to say that Salvation Army leaders are conscious of the odds against them more than most, for in the main they serve the poorest and least literate sections of the community. There is little social advantage to be gained by becoming a Christian in India today. The scales are weighted against such a decision. But if the members of the conference took a long hard look at the obstacles in their way, they did not forget the promise of their Lord ever to be with them.

Four months later the Commissioner was in Madras again representing the General—this time at the retirement of Colonel and Mrs James Kennedy, two Scottish officers who entered the work in 1946 and had given all but four years of their service to India.

From there it was but a short run to Bapatla where, at 10 o'clock on a weekday morning, a capacity congregation filled the hall for the installation of the first Telegu officer to be entrusted with the responsibility of territorial leadership. The meeting hailed this with unrestrained delight and almost smothered their new leader with their enthusiastic garlanding. Repeatedly members of the congregation rose to their feet to ask for a minute—'only a minute'—to add their personal tribute to the worth of Colonel Mannam Samuel. One divisional commander went so far as to say that 'after 93 years our leaders have found a diamond in the territory'. It testifies to the Commissioner's strength of will, as well as to her sense of the fitness of things, that she gave her prepared Bible message and delivered the General's charge before calling upon the Colonel to respond to the acclamations with which he had been greeted.

The end of September 1975 saw Calliss in London—this time to attend the Commissioners' and territorial commanders' conference held from 26 September to 6 October under the presidency of General Clarence Wiseman. This was a particularly valuable experience for she found herself one of the 86 delegates drawn from 40 territories and commands covering 56 countries. The whole range of evangelical enterprise came under consideration. Christian ethical standards were both discussed and reaffirmed, and considerable time was given to the relationship of The Salvation Army with the Christian churches in general. In its final conclusions (summarized in *The War Cry* for 25 October 1975), the conference declared that 'the life and structure of the whole church of Christ is a matter of concern to the Army'.

Where Christian believers are in a minority—as they are throughout Asia—the churches are on much closer terms than in the west where the Christian community, enjoying a statistical majority, tends to be more concerned about the differences which exist between the faithful. Elsewhere such luxuries are too costly for minority groups to afford. So while in Indonesia Calliss sought—and indeed succeeded—in strengthening the Army's standing with the Ministry of Religious Affairs, thus confirming a Moslem government's faith in the integrity of a Christian body in the task of human caring without regard for creed or colour.

In Sri Lanka she became vice-president of the National Christian Council and also served on the executive of the Sinhalese Bible Society, so that she was more than happy to be appointed as one of the seven-member Salvation Army delegation to the Fifth Assembly of the World Council of Churches meeting in Nairobi from 23 November to 10 December of that year.

There had always been a weighty delegation from the Army at each successive World Assembly from 1948 onwards. On this occasion there was an even more balanced representation because, for the first time, two soldiers were included in addition to the five officers. The leader was Commissioner H. W. G. Williams, OBE, FRCS, FCIS (International Headquarters), supported by Commissioner Gladys Calliss (Sri Lanka), Colonel Ernest Denham (International Headquarters), Colonel Joshua Ngugi (East Africa), Lieut.-Colonel Thorsten Kjäll (Sweden), Mrs Grace Lodge (United States) and Sister Anwyn Dumbleton (United Kingdom).

Calliss had spent the greater part of her officership in the Third World, so her cup of joy was running over to see her beloved Salvationists carrying themselves so handsomely in the very heart of that world. She profited by the many enriching contacts—formal and informal—made with friend and stranger, and no churchman who fell into conversation with her could fail to be impressed by this mature woman whose approach to the problems of human need had for so long been rooted in personal experience. She shared in the Assembly's various acts of public witness, marked the strengths—and the weaknesses—of the lengthy discussions, attended the Salvation Army holiness meeting on the Sunday where over 1,000 Africans were present and, at the public gathering in the Uhuru park, watched the Nairobi Central Band, headed by its tall African bandmaster, lead the long processional columns into place with what was described as 'perfect step and impeccable timing'. She echoed the judgement of a fellow delegate who said that his experiences at Nairobi made him a better Salvationist.

After these unforgettable days Calliss had almost to scurry back to Colombo where on 25 February 1976, General and Mrs Wiseman arrived at the Bandaranaike international airport, and then received a public welcome in the William Booth Memorial Hall. The next day the General and his wife met the leading officers of the territory in fellowship, and also conducted two sessions of officers' councils. On the Saturday the hall was filled to capacity with home league members to greet Mrs Wiseman, and later with young people present to listen to the General as well.

Sunday was spent at Rambukkana, an important provincial town in the virtual centre of the island, where two meetings had been arranged. Three large elephants walked in front of the march carrying banners bearing the current slogan: 'Share your Faith'. Colombo Central Band supplied the music to which national dancers, corps cadets, adherents, home league members, soldiers young and old, marched along the gaily decorated road leading to the Booth-Tucker hall, where the international visitors were accorded the honour of a 'Pavada'—or white cloth welcome. Army friends were present in goodly numbers with the Anglican Archbishop of Kurunegala on the platform. But both morning and afternoon gatherings were profoundly spiritual occasions, and no one rejoiced more than Calliss when there were seekers at the Mercy Seat in both meetings.

Yet beyond the glamour of the crowds and the much less glamorous attention to detail which such efforts demand, Calliss never lost her interest in people—particularly her officers and, of that group, those who were serving in lands other than their own because they felt this to be the will of the Lord for them. She shared fellowship that year with some of them when she took her furlough at Coonoor in the Nilgiri Hills in southern India where the Army had a holiday home. The customary resorts were beyond the frugal allowances of missionary officers, so from all parts of the sub-continent westerners—Americans, Europeans, Australians—made their way each year to 'Surrenden'. The bonus was that many of the officers' children attended school either at 'Hebron' at Coonoor, or 'Lushington' further up the hills at Ootacamund. So one or both parents would plan to attend the celebrations at the end of the school year, and then parents and children could enjoy their annual holiday together.

Calliss had been a leader long enough to be aware of the tensions which can arise when the claims of duty conflict with those of the family. One day while on furlough she stayed indoors instead of going off on the planned excursion, and this gave her an opportunity of hearing again at first hand about this often hidden—and sometimes forgotten—aspect of Salvation Army life.

For example, for parents stationed in Pakistan or northern India, Coonoor was the nearest school within their price range where a western education was obtainable. There was nothing whatever amiss with this arrangement save the distance of the separation. It was not the fault of the school staff that children missed their parents. It would have been unnatural had they not. Nor were parents to be blamed because their children were constantly in their thoughts. Again, it would have been unnatural were they not. But a mother was called upon to do despite to one of her deepest natural instincts when, at the moment of parting, she had to force perhaps the youngest in her family to let go her hand—and then quickly vanish from sight lest the child make one more vain attempt to cling to her.

Such separation became most distressing of all when India and Pakistan were at war. Without warning parents found that they could not go to their children at the annual holiday time, nor could their children come to them. Direct posts were suspended between the two countries. Even when life is normal the distances involved are almost beyond the comprehension of those of us living on the tight little island known as Britain. Maybe the silver lining to this cloud in the family sky is the natural resilience of most children, and the kindness of officers near at hand who would stand in for the parents. They themselves had learned from experience where to find the grace to bear the burdens which their personal dedication involves. Calliss had a profound faith in guardian angels, especially where missionary officers' children were concerned. Without doubt many of those angels have a human form and human hands and a loving human concern!

Later that same year Calliss received the news which she had been partly expecting, partly fearing, but for which she had been partly preparing. She would be farewelling from Sri Lanka at the end of January, 1977, and would be retiring from active service as an officer on 1 July of that year.

Her immediate reaction was to address herself with renewed vigour to matters of unfinished business. There was already a home for elderly women in Colombo, and similar accommodation had been opened more recently for men, but so far there was no adequate provision for retired officers. It was the Commissioner's special joy to lay the foundation stone for the first of two homes to be erected for this purpose.

Her own long-term plans for the development of the Sinhalese officers included another three-day residential seminar at the Weerasooriya Conference Centre, followed by a visit from the ever helpful international secretary, Commissioner Arthur Hook, accompanied this time by Mrs Hook, to lead a series of councils with the entire officer corps.

The Christmas season was quickly upon her with its remembrance of the needy, its parties for children, its augmented feeding programme for the hungry, its care for the lonely and the aged—all in remembrance of the birth of Him in whose name these works of love and mercy were carried out. The watchnight meeting followed within the week and another eager congregation filled the William Booth Memorial Hall. Inevitably each event in this unending round was led or addressed by Calliss—sometimes both!

A new session of cadets was welcomed at the training college on 13 January 1977 and then on January 28 came her public farewell, presided over by the Bishop of Colombo, the Rt Rev C. L. Abeynaike, with numerous civic and religious leaders sharing the platform, including the president of the Methodist Church and the general secretary of the Bible Society. Her stay in Sri Lanka had lasted but little over three years, but her command had gained her the respect of all who knew her, and her kindness had won their hearts. 'Our dear Commissioner' was the phrase applied to her in the press report of her final meetings.

Calliss stayed long enough in Colombo to welcome her successor—another Australian, Colonel Eva Burrows—as territorial commander in her place, after which she left immediately for Singapore and Jakarta. The remaining months were to be a kind of epilogue, but a happy and rewarding epilogue, to her life of service to God and the Army.

14

No rocking chair required!

WITH Sri Lanka now behind her there were but five months of active service left for Calliss. However, they were to be five full months. Any other kind of months—or minutes for that matter—had no place in her schedule. To begin by spending the opening weeks of those final months in Java was just the kind of stimulus she needed to take the final home run in her stride.

Indonesia was her second motherland. She had lived there for more than a quarter of a century. She knew the language as well as any national. She needed no interpreter either in private conversation or public meeting. She had trained virtually all the younger officers. There was hardly a corps or social institution which she had not visited. These people were her people and her God was their God, even though so many of them did not know Him by the name which she used in her prayers. So conferences and discussions were not ordeals which she dreaded but occasions when she could rejoice with her Salvationist comrades over the blessings which had been theirs, and in faith could anticipate those which God would yet shower upon them. So after seasons of rich fellowship of heart and mind enjoyed in both East and West Java alike, this happy band of officers returned to their various appointments while Calliss left for Australia.

This meant still more days of delight for her. It was eight years since she had stood beside the river red gum in Adelaide's Botanic Park where Gore and Saunders had held their first open-air meeting, and there had been many more changes still since she had said her first goodbye to the Commonwealth in 1947. The capital cities had grown by leaps and bounds. Their suburbs had spread beyond all recognition. Their streets were more crowded. Pedestrians—and motorists—lived more dangerously. But the sound of the kookaburra could still be heard in the land; the southerly buster still blew; even the coastal scrub retained its attractive colouring, while the coolness of the breaking surf remained a welcome distraction in the heat of the day. But of still greater delight to Calliss was the opportunity of renewed fellowship with her contemporaries from training days.

Her first pilgrimage was to Canberra where her fellow cadets of the Faith Session had arranged a welcome home for her. More than 60 of them were present—counting husbands and/or wives who, by reason of marriage, had become honorary members of the session. Now more than 40 years on all but half-a-dozen were retired. Time had laid her unforgiving finger on more than a few so that recognition was not always instantaneous. In spite of the hazards of her overseas service Calliss had been more kindly treated than most. But their assembled zeal was as fresh as ever and, before they parted, they joined in the singing of their favourite sessional chorus:

> Reckon on me following Thee,
> Living for ever Thy servant to be;
> Cloudy or fine, Lord, I am Thine,
> Until Thy face I shall see.

Theirs had never been a committal for a fixed period only. It was always as long as life shall last.

Refreshed and renewed, Calliss pressed on to Sydney and Newcastle and, at the former, was able to attend the public welcome of the new session of cadets, as well as to greet a woman-cadet from Indonesia who had been sent to Australia to complete the second half of her training.

Then across to the west where she revisited some of the scenes of her early officership in the 1930s—only now she was returning as one of the principal speakers at the state congress in Perth. There are at least six annual congresses of this kind in the Commonwealth, and Australian Salvationists never seem to weary of these yearly events. Flags fly, bands play, the timbrels are to the fore, young and old join in the marches, congregations fill the largest available halls, and the congress leader has not to lament the lack of response but rather to discover how best to employ the gifts of those who dedicate themselves to the Lord's service.

The same kind of experience, only on an even higher note, was repeated when Calliss crossed the Nullabor Plain to share in the congress in Adelaide. This was her home, and this particular Sunday the 50th anniversary of the actual day when the Goodwood band had marched through the Colonel Light Gardens suburb announcing the opening of a new Salvation Army corps. The local press described Calliss as a wanderer returning home. If so, her wandering had not been aimless but to good purpose—and so continued, for no sooner were the Adelaide gatherings concluded than she left to conduct Easter meetings in New Zealand. Here she was welcomed by a missionary-minded people and taken to see the progress made in one of the Army's latest openings in the South Pacific—the island of Fiji. Thence she moved on to the Philippines where she found herself in a setting that was not unfamiliar. She was in the tropics; another woman leader—Lieut.-Colonel Ingrid Lindberg—stood beside her; this time an interpreter was required but, as so often had happened in the past, the word had free course and was glorified.

As soon as this further campaign was over Calliss left for London to attend the public welcome to the High Council assembled, on Thursday 28 April 1977, to elect a successor to General Clarence Wiseman. She was one of the three women members of the council and was elected to serve as one of the three tellers. This was the second election which she had attended and so was no stranger to the procedures to be followed. As in previous years the business on hand was neither hurried nor delayed. Time was neither stinted nor wasted. The rule that the successful nominee should receive two-thirds of the votes cast was met at the first ballot, and on 5 May Commissioner Arnold Brown was announced as the General-elect.

The end of her active officership was now in sight for Calliss and she took a fortnight's break in Scotland—well deserved after the strain of the ceaseless round of meetings which had been hers since leaving Sri Lanka at the beginning of the year. But where was she going to live after having been away from her native land since July 1947? No use denying that this question had been on her mind even while she was still in Sri Lanka. The allowances received by a single woman missionary officer—even though a territorial leader—had been insufficient to enable her to save enough to put down a deposit in the normal way on the most modest dwelling. Beside not even her spartan lifestyle had endeared to her the one room, one window and one door pattern of unit which, in some quarters, is regarded as adequate for a single senior citizen. She was not in the habit of crying for the moon but she was not enamoured of being so fenced in.

There was, however, in one of Adelaide's green and pleasant suburbs, not far from Colonel Light Gardens, a delightful home for senior citizens, graded to suit the varying needs of the various occupants. A veteran women's social officer lived in one of these self-contained flats which was also linked to the main building by bell and telephone in case of emergency. One like that, murmured Calliss to herself and, as had been her lifelong habit, she took her need to the Lord in prayer.

Meanwhile her retirement meeting in the Melbourne Temple drew near. The Territorial Commander (Commissioner W. R. H. Goodier) was to preside. The Melbourne Staff Band occupied the platform. By a happy coincidence the current leaders of the Army's work in Indonesia—Colonel and Mrs Edwin Marion, themselves Australians—were home on furlough and were present as well. The Colonel spoke bringing Indonesia's tribute. Lieut.-Colonel Walter Hull, Editor-in-Chief in Melbourne, who himself belonged to the Colonel Light Gardens Corps as a young Salvationist, paid Australia's tribute. When the band brought their benediction with the selection 'His Guardian Care', Calliss felt that all that could be said had been said. One of the cadets present did not entirely share this view and, before leaving, approached her with a small but tastefully wrapped gift. She would look at it later.

Now what about a place for Calliss to lay her head? Even that hope was to be realized, for the current occupant of the flat she had so greatly admired felt that, at 90 years of age, she could no longer look after herself. She had therefore asked for a transfer to the hostel section of the home but on second thoughts—or prompted by some happy inspiration, which is what a second thought can be—said that, if it was the same to everybody else, she would stay in her flat for the moment and keep it warm for Commissioner Calliss. So for the first time since she had left home as a girl, Calliss had now a place of her own. Not just one door, one window and one room either but two doors, four windows and two verandahs, together with a pocket handkerchief-sized lawn, smooth as a billiard table, surrounded by a flower bedecked border. After 30 years of using dippers and buckets and broad shallow pans, here was a gleaming white bath with both hot and cold at the turn of a tap. And a shower for good measure!

Calliss wandered round her compact and comfortable domain as one entranced. How was she going to cope with all these gadgets? Even the washing machine looked formidable. Which button did what? But the resourcefulness which had helped her to adapt to the primitive conditions of central Sulawesi, now enabled her to re-adapt to the more sophisticated life of a modern Australian city. Soon she was wheeling her trolley along the broad aisles of the local super-market, gazing to the right and to the left at the shelves packed with farmhouse cheese, freshly cut celery and appetizing wholemeal bread—delights to which she had long been a stranger—but here present in such abundance that to buy what she needed was not to deny any other shopper what he or she wanted.

As for work to do, she discovered it was possible to be as busy in retirement as ever she had been while on active service. Whether it was wise to continue at such a pace was another matter. But meetings of all kinds are ever holding out both hands to any speaker who had something to say and knew how to say it. Groups in one half of the world are eager to learn how the other half lives. Salvation Army corps have an insatiable appetite for 'specials'. The one-time girl corps cadet who had made good was not to be allowed to remain idle. Indeed, it was not long before Calliss became President of the Retired Officers' Fellowship in South Australia and all her skills as a training officer came into their own when these veterans went out on their country campaigns. Soon Calliss was having to keep as close a watch on her engagement calendar now that she was at home as ever she did when she was overseas. But for her all these activities became vantage points from which she pleaded the cause of those with whom she had worked formerly and who would always remain her fellow labourers in the Lord. So parcels of reading matter for English-speaking missionaries overseas were continually being dispatched from the Kingswood post office on the Unley Road. Materials for sales of work in Colombo were neatly parcelled together. Delicacies unobtainable in central Sulawesi were posted to expatriate officers in that area. Aids for officer training were added to goodies not to be found on institutional menus in Java. And in any spare moment there was always her dream flat to keep spotless and shining. The doorway bore the legend 'Damai Sentosa'. Both were Indonesian words and meant 'Peace and Rest', but 'Sentosa' was also used in the Sinhalese tongue and meant 'happiness'. It was her continued activity which kept Calliss as happy at the end of the road as at the beginning. Retirement for her did not mean the doubtful blessing of having nothing to do. That was closer to death than life.

She thought again of the present which she had been given at the close of her retirement meeting in Melbourne. Made of a rare Tasmanian wood—so she was told—and very fragile. When the tiny parcel was opened there lay snugly inside—a miniature rocking chair.

A witty present for which she was grateful and, what was more, she knew what to do with it. It was placed as an ornament on her mantelpiece. Even in retirement she had no use for a rocking chair!